'An antidote to the ⎯⎯⎯⎯⎯ ⎯. This is an honest, warm an ⎯⎯⎯⎯⎯⎯⎯ n... one bird at a time.' **Nick Baker, naturalist and TV presenter**

'This is a generous, honest and gently inspirational book, a touching exploration of the solace we find in neighbourhood nature. Beginners at birdwatching and beginners at life – all of us – can learn something from Joe Harkness.' **Patrick Barkham, author of *Islander***

'A gripping, funny, moving and at times brutally honest account of a life spent on the edge, and how one man's passion for birds helped him deal with life's problems. One of the most important books I have read for a long time.' **Stephen Moss, author of *The Robin: A Biography***

'A manifesto for transformation ... Inclusive, unpretentious and evangelical in the best way.' **Melissa Harrison, author of *All Among the Barley***

'Nature cannot cure you, but reading this beautiful and honest book will take you very close indeed to the best things going.' **Tim Dee, author of *The Running Sky***

'The effect of *Bird Therapy* is to fling open a window onto the sky, the garden, the hedge, the sea – wherever you are, onto a very modern mindfulness. It's a real tonic; a prescription, a guide and a hopeful way to soar.' **Nicola Chester, nature writer and the RSPB's longest-running female columnist**

Joe Harkness has been running his Bird Therapy blog for the last four years, where he writes openly about his wellbeing and his connection with the outdoors. He also speaks publicly about his mental health in the hope of helping others with theirs. As well as writing for numerous publications, he has appeared on BBC's *Winterwatch* alongside Chris Packham, discussing male suicide. He is a Special Educational Needs Coordinator and has worked with vulnerable groups for ten years.

@birdtherapy
www.birdtherapy.blog

BIRD THERAPY

With special thanks to
Bill Bailey
Adam Huttly
Deb Jordan, Pensthorpe Natural Park

Bird
Therapy

Joe Harkness

unbound

First published in 2019
This paperback edition first published in 2020

Unbound
6th Floor Mutual House, 70 Conduit Street, London W1S 2GF

www.unbound.com

Text Design by PDQ

Illustrations © Jo Brown

A CIP record for this book is available from the British Library

ISBN 978-1-78352-898-1 (paperback)
ISBN 978-1-78352-772-4 (hardback)
ISBN 978-1-78352-774-8 (ebook)

Printed and bound in Great Britain by Clays Ltd, Elcograf S.p.A.

1 3 5 7 9 8 6 4 2

This book is dedicated to the loving memory of my aunties, Julie and Ruth. Both believed in me and both believed in the power of nature.

Contents

Foreword

We bump, we bruise, we scrape and graze, we nick, cut, slice and slash our flesh, we bleed. We ache, we sweat, we vomit. We band-aid, we bandage, we medicate. We have surgery. And all of that is fine. It's everyday, it's normal, it's acceptable. Even when we cry about it, sympathy comes rushing up to tell us that it will be okay.

'Last weekend I fell off a ladder and ripped my arm open. I needed thirty stitches and now I'm on antibiotics…'
'Oh that's awful, is there anything I can do to help?'

'Last weekend I was hopelessly depressed, so I strung up a sheet to the rafters and tried to hang myself…'

Silence, or shock, or nothing, because the likelihood of actually saying that is almost nil. Because even now, in the twenty-first century, mental health is still steeped in a lethal taboo which locks sick people up in themselves and leads to tragedy. The day I tied the rope, estimated its stretch and used a tape to measure the drop – but didn't kill myself – I had three 'normal' telephone calls with friends and family. And none of them had any idea what had so nearly happened – because I had no capacity to tell them. There was no bridge, no angle, no route to that discussion because my agony was 'not allowed'. I was a boy, and 'boys don't cry', men can't fail; we have to be strong. Our lips can't quiver, they have to be stiff and upper. But that is all so obviously wrong, and the cost is immeasurable. The unacceptable male suicide rates in the UK are sadly only part of a desperate mental health crisis.

My dogs saved me. A human saved Joe Harkness, and this is his story. It will be hailed as 'brave', 'courageous' or 'bold'. It's not; he's not. It's simply true and he is simply honest. He has told his harrowing and reassuring and wonderful story full-frontal, cleverly, articulately, essentially and creatively. His journey is a map of recovery and understanding, and its graphic presence will undoubtedly serve as a template for others to find respite, through seemingly unlikely means – a connection with nature, a love of birds. But if this strikes you as a quirky, niche therapy with little real world application then read on. Joe spells it out frankly but critically, qualifies it with authority, and presents a very compelling case for the efficacy of natural health.

I read lots. Bad, good, interesting, important and occasionally brilliant books. I can't remember the last book that I read that I could say with absolute assurance would save lives. But this one will. So from my perspective that makes it an exceptional book. Thank you, Joe; you are a top bloke, a real human – not brave, but rare.

Chris Packham
New Forest

I.

A breakdown, a buzzard and the Broads

2013. The bedsheet was twisted as tight as I could physically wrench it and tied off tightly on to one of the beams above. In the absence of any rope, or rationality, it would have to do. Standing astride the hollow loft hatch, I looked through the small black void into the hallway below, but could hardly see anything. Life presented itself in silhouettes, formless shapes viewed through tear-burned eyes. I no longer wanted to be here anymore. I no longer wanted to be anywhere. It wasn't the first time I'd been in this place, but every time, I wanted it to be the last.

I yanked the makeshift noose to check its tightness and started to place it around my neck; it felt soft and warm where I'd twisted it, in contrast to the stony coldness in my mind. The serene silence was broken by a door opening, frightened shouting and footsteps, running up the stairs. An interruption – how untimely – stern and caring words, urging me to stop. I was talked down, quite literally, and pleaded with to consider the wider implications of my actions upon other people – but I couldn't. It was evident that I needed help, but I continued to do all I could to avoid getting any.

Upon reading these opening paragraphs, I implore you not to think that this book is going be a solemn read; I promise that *Bird Therapy* is a positive tale. It's a joyous journal, charting how the discovery of birdwatching transformed my life for the better. That moment was to be a turning point in my life and the catalyst for this book. This – my mental health – is the first of the two elements that form the story of *Bird Therapy* and in order for my story to spread its metaphorical wings, we have to start at the bottom.

Four months after this emotional nadir and I was hungry. On the cobbled streets of Norwich are many places to devour a full English breakfast, in fact so many that we even have our own fry-up inspector. There I sat, guzzling artisan bacon alongside two of my friends, lining our stomachs in preparation for the annual Norwich beer festival. In this chic café, all mahogany chairs and chalkboard menus, I admitted to 'outsiders', for the first time, that there was something wrong with my mental health. It was a heady moment and it felt like a proverbial weight had been lifted from my mind. The dirty little secret I'd been lugging around and hiding away was finally out in the open.

I ploughed into the festival with renewed optimism, masking my actual fragility with copious amounts of real ale, as I'd long conditioned myself to do. As the afternoon drinking session drew to a close, we made the decision to walk to a nearby pub to continue imbibing, but I was nearing a point I knew all too well – the point where

I lose all inhibition, self-control and awareness. After a short while and a few pints, a gentleman approached me at the bar and asked me if I was related to my father – stating how much I looked like him when he was younger and what a 'great guy' he was when he knew him. My inebriated self snapped back at him, snarling and sniping that I didn't want to know anything about him and was *nothing* like him.

Twenty-five years of suppressed hurt, confusion and despondency bubbled up to the surface and I imploded. I couldn't cope with someone challenging the lifetime of negativity that I'd bred inside my head, as far as my father was concerned. A stranger was telling me that my dad, who I believed to be a monster, was actually a decent bloke. No one had the right to undermine what I believed, no one, and this threw me into a maelstrom of emotions. I had to get out. 'I'm going for a fag,' I lied, and I left the pub without telling anyone and walked, spiralling further downwards inside.

I didn't realise it, but this was the onset of a nervous breakdown and it would have to get worse before I could start to get better. I was made safe that night, tucked in like a toddler and watched until I went to sleep. When I woke though, my mind was rushing and my thoughts were reeling – the uncontrollable culmination of years of negative thinking. There was no rationalisation and no control, meaning that I shook, sobbed and clutched at my temples, urging it all to go away, as if rubbing my head would help.

An emergency doctor's appointment was booked and there began my journey to recovery.

The first thing the doctor did was to sign me off work for an indefinite period of time – adding my name to the ever-growing waiting list for mental health support in Norfolk. I remember sitting in a bright clinical room and trying to explain the issues and feelings I'd been experiencing for most of my adult life. I felt stupid and even a little bit scared, trying to describe my thought processes out loud, as if expressing them verbally somehow made them more real. I shared that I'd been self-medicating since roughly the age of fifteen, firstly with daily cannabis use and then with a daily cocktail of other illegal drugs, and alcohol, from my late teens until my mid-twenties. I told the doctor I was convinced my mind was already fragile prior to this, but sitting there and baring my soul to her, that fragility had fractured completely – I had finally accepted that I needed help.

She diagnosed me with Obsessive Compulsive Disorder (OCD) and Generalised Anxiety Disorder (GAD), based on my descriptions of how I thought and felt. These are just words though, labels, and everyone experiences mental health issues on an individual basis. Sometimes I feel bloody awesome and like I can achieve anything, yet other times I hate everyone and everything and just want to be on my own. This is different for everyone and it's so important to recognise when people are struggling, like other people had with me.

With this in mind, it's ridiculously difficult to describe what it's like to live with chronic anxiety to anyone who hasn't been exposed to it themselves in some way. The point is, it may be my experience of anxiety, but it's unlikely to be the same as anyone else's. It may be similar, we may share traits and symptoms, but as we're so often told, we're all 'wired differently'. Anyway, I'll give it a go.

My own anxiety manifests in a constant, nagging feeling that I've done something wrong or am about to do so. To me, badness and wrongness are disastrous; I need everything to be safe and controlled. I constantly worry about every action, decision, word or behaviour that I undertake, leading me to plan and organise everything that I can – in minute detail.

Invariably, I then start to dwell on this feeling and what may have caused it and so begins a cycle of negative thinking. I worry intensely about what other people think of me; I'm persistently paranoid and will repeat events and conversations over and over in my mind, convinced that I've said or done something bad. This leaves me feeling constantly on edge and hyper-aware of how I interact with people, having a knock-on effect on my concentration and enjoyment of life in general – bang goes the positivity!

I sweat, I shake, I fret and I ache, but time has enabled me to learn what the warning signs are and calm myself enough to function; for example, in a supermarket or other public place. I thought I could mask the anxiety with alcohol or drugs, but this was a figment of my past and not my present. Anxiety follows me everywhere and sometimes it gets so intense that it hurts my head, gives me a headache and keeps me awake at night. My OCD is even harder to explain, but likewise, I'll give it a go.

The 'O' in OCD stands for obsessive. Obsession, for me, means that everything needs to be a certain way; arranged a certain way, done in a certain way – it's all about order. Without order, bad things will happen, but I'm never really sure what those bad things are, I just know it will. I can't really explain what the particular 'way' is either, as it's more to do with how my methodologies feel; certain ways of doing things feel safe, right and secure. I like to make lists and plan every aspect of my life, something explored further in this book. I call this process 'mapping'. This quest for ideal circumstance and perfection isn't worth the time I spend searching for it, as I know I can't prepare for every eventuality, but it certainly makes me feel better.

I combat anxieties with rituals that make me feel at ease. At the minute, I'm struggling with social media use, and I alleviate this by pinching and biting the skin on my fingers. I've always done this for as long as I can remember, but it's worsened recently and unfortunately, my fingers and nails are now a bit of a mess and the skin on my face isn't great either. This is what the 'C' stands for – compulsive – and I have plenty of compulsive behaviours, some rational and some ridiculous. The worst was a long-standing fear of incontinence in public and therefore planning every aspect of my life around the availability of toilet facilities. It got so bad that I would go to the toilet for the sake of going, not because I actually needed to. Thankfully, I've managed to overcome this now, but there's still a residual need to over-visit bathrooms lingering in my subconscious.

The next step the doctor took was to prescribe me antidepressants from the selective serotonin reuptake inhibitor (SSRI) family. These are taken to increase the levels of serotonin in the brain, lifting overall mood; however, in my case, I was prescribed them to help with my thought processes and OCD. My initial thoughts were that I wasn't keen to take any medication and most of this mindset came from the stigma surrounding antidepressant medication. I wanted to take ownership of my mental health and challenge it myself. At this time though, I needed to make instant changes to try and settle down my mind and after much deliberation, I started a low dose of Sertraline to try and 'take the edge off' the way I felt.

I ended up taking three weeks off work and it was during this time that the first of two experiences occurred, which bedded in the roots of Bird Therapy.

I started going walking, to get me out of the house and exercising. I'd read that exercise and fresh air were two of the best activities I could do to help improve my wellbeing. My partner and I found a booklet of circular walks in Norfolk and were working our way through some of them. It was on one of these walks, a North Walsham to

Felmingham circuit, that I experienced the origins of my Bird Therapy.

It began as we stepped out on to an open field, lined with horizontal, stubbled furrows resembling rippled wavelets. The path split the field in two, forming a green artery straight through it, disappearing on the other side where it was swallowed by the tree line. As we crossed this open ground, a large bird appeared above the trees, soaring. A strange, slurred mewing sound emanated from it. It held me rapt, bulky and brown, with white barring on its wings – a common buzzard, or *Buteo buteo* to give it its Linnaean name. 'Look at that buzzard,' I exclaimed to my partner, somehow knowing exactly what it was.

Regal and enchanting, it dipped down and disappeared below the tree line, only to rise again, circling and gliding on outstretched, v-shaped wings. It represented so much to me in that moment: it represented freedom and it represented hope. On that day, I wasn't entirely sure how, but deep in my subconscious lay an understanding that I knew this bird. I couldn't get it out of my mind and I wanted to experience that feeling again.

As I look back now, I can appreciate how I knew it was a buzzard; an interest in the natural world had been ingrained in my psyche from a young age. As a child, I spent most of my time outdoors – whether out with friends, walking with family or playing in my grandparents' cottage-style garden – I loved it. I grew up in an era when it was still 'safe' to go out all day and play – back when you were sent out in the morning and told to be back for tea at six. Yes, I played football and rode pushbikes around, but I also built dens, climbed trees and embraced the freedom that we had been granted.

At the age of four my parents separated, and my mother and I moved to Brundall in Norfolk to live with my grandparents. In the absence of a father, I spent a lot of time with my grandfather, or 'Pops' as I call him nowadays. He grew up in North Wales and then on a houseboat in Brundall, and as a result he's always held a close affinity with rivers and the Norfolk Broads. He's a quiet and thoughtful man with a great passion for the outdoors, a keen eye for wildlife and a calming way of explaining the wonders of nature.

In the hot summer months, we used to spend time at Salhouse Broad, on a boat which belonged to a friend of my grandparents. The adventure always began by parking at the public car park. Dark and shaded, it was surrounded by seemingly ancient trees and however hot it was outside of this dim vacuum, it was always cooler as you strolled down to the broad itself. A ten-minute walk followed, meandering along stretches of muddy pathways and boardwalk. Periodically along the route, gnarled trees stood with huge chunks missing. Although devoid of life, I would breathe it back into them by running and dancing around their cocoon-like trunks. Woodland became nettle bed, which then became reed bed. Occasionally sunlight would filter through, vitalising the murk with glittering cascades of green and gold.

Towards the end of the path, soil turned to sand and the vegetation began to open out, offering options. Here you had to make a choice – boardwalk or broad walk? The pull of the open water usually outweighed any other option here – so it was broad walk. I ran free, up the hill that borders the south edge of the broad. Onward and through the prickly thicket, a rabbit run forged by decades of gambolling children. Upon reaching the apex point, I would become the captain of the broad, looking down across the surface and surveying the dayboats dotting the water and the families frolicking below on the sandy edge. It was a picture-postcard scene; it was Norfolk in a nutshell.

My grandparents' friends used to moor up at the water's edge on the south side of the broad and it was from here that we would board the great ship. The water always seemed crystalline and clean, unaffected by the algal growth that's present today. The boat was the setting for the first steps in my avian tutelage, where my water-based lessons in recognising the commonest wildfowl began. We started with simple and easy-to-remember birds: mute swans, coots and moorhens. All predominantly one colour, although the larger coot with its white bill, versus the more compact, red-and-yellow-beaked moorhen, was the first differential between bird species that I learned.

What was the slender-necked, regal-looking bird that kept diving below the broad's surface? A flash of dazzling white leading up to a ruffled rufous lion's mane, satin-white face and sharp grey bill. What was this handsome creature, darting and diving around us? My grandfather told me what it was – another species I would be able to identify forever, unmistakable and elegant: a great crested grebe. He'd tell me about kingfishers and their beguiling, azure beauty. We never saw one, but I dreamed of the day I would see my first. Would it be fishing? Would I be able to watch it properly? He'd started my interest in nature in an organic and easy way; it wasn't forced and I grew to love the outdoors much in the same way as he did.

We would drive around the country lanes of Norfolk – he was a carpenter and work could be anywhere in our sparse county. This gave us the opportunity to look at other birds as we travelled around and this was where I first saw the fluttering falcon, that hovering hawk – a kestrel. 'What's that there?' There was a small bird, seemingly suspended in the air, on rapidly beating wings, suddenly dropping, before rising again – not quite as high as it first was. 'That's a kestrel,' he told me. 'They hover like that because they're looking for mice to swoop down on and catch.' This dainty and graceful bird was actually a ruthless hunter. I would learn, later, about how kestrels fly into the wind and channel it to enable themselves to linger in the air, fastened like puppets on a string. Now, whenever I see one hovering by the roadside, these memories stir.

Almost everybody who I've met who knew me as a child has stated that I was inquisitive to the point of incessantly irritating – and sifting through old school reports, I'm disheartened to read what I was like in class. I disrupted other children's learning, demanded the teacher's attention constantly and sought acceptance through negative behaviour. As a teacher who works with lots of young people with behavioural difficulties, I often wonder if I slipped under the behavioural radar at primary school. A lot of my behaviour back then bore the warning signs of future mental unsteadiness. For as long as I can remember, I've been interested in 'odd' topics and have often fixated on quite specific areas of interest; perhaps this was an early sign of the future OCD me? I was sociable but somewhat antisocial, trapped in my microcosmic hobbies; informed yet confused.

Primary school was, however, a further catalyst for my interest in nature. This was greatly encouraged by the head teacher, Mr Capp – a strong advocate for the natural beauty of the county of Norfolk. He took his zeal for the area to the next level and was so keen on the importance of learning about the history and wildlife of the Norfolk Broads that he facilitated the creation of our own school broad.

An area of unused and overgrown grassland at the bottom of our 'paddock' was flattened and landscaped. A pit was dug, lined and filled, before being screened with vegetation. Finally, a length of boardwalk was placed along one edge, creating the ultimate on-site field-study centre. Can you imagine that at the end of your school playing field? This only served to enhance my appreciation of the Norfolk countryside, providing immediate access to something we would usually have to travel to, to experience.

Mr Capp was also famed for his field trips, and I distinctly remember visiting How Hill, an environmental study centre near Ludham. A lot of attention was placed on the supposedly haunted dormitory – room thirteen – but my attention was elsewhere. How Hill was my dream, green classroom, fully immersed in nature. Amidst the clamour of pond dipping and our excited observations of water boatmen, we met the iconic Eric 'The Marshman' Edwards.

I was struck by this leather-skinned and red-cheeked workhorse of a man, whose broad Norfolk accent told us, in no uncertain terms, how to correctly scythe reed and sedge. In 2012 he passed away, leaving behind a legacy of true-Norfolk tales and ways. I read that he once told Baroness Margaret Thatcher that she was 'doing it wrong' when he was giving her a thatching demonstration – one of few people ever to challenge her authority.

The trip to How Hill, at the age of ten, left me with firmly entrenched memories of just how beautiful the Norfolk Broads could be. A daydream could lead to me visualising that sweeping view across the reed beds again, the skyline punctuated by the monochromatic skeleton of the Clayrack drainage mill. Now I'm older I cherish these vistas even more – they epitomise Norfolk's natural and agricultural history. In the follow-up art project that we did in class, I tried to recreate one of these panoramas in a mock-Impressionist style. My mother found the project whilst moving home recently, and, well, it looked a lot better when I was younger.

The second experience that forged Bird Therapy was one that re-energised my long-suppressed interest in birdwatching. It involved my grandfather and a belated birthday present. This wasn't a childhood occurrence, in fact it happened in July 2014, only nine months after my breakdown. Being particularly unmaterialistic, Pops could be a difficult person to buy presents for. This year, though, I had an idea, which if he was happy to oblige would surpass any physical gift. We discussed it over the phone: 'How about I take you out for lunch somewhere, then we could go for a walk and do some birdwatching?' He said that he'd love to do just that and that it was a fantastic idea – so we agreed a date and I said I'd ponder on our destination.

I'd been informed by a friend that the Norfolk Wildlife Trust (NWT) ran daily boat trips on Hickling Broad. It was something I'd looked into doing on my own and, indeed, it seemed like the perfect day out for me and Pops. The boat trip meant meeting at a specified mooring spot, to join a small group and be ferried out across broad and backwater by an expert guide. There were two stop-off points: a sixty-foot viewing tower and a bird hide that was only accessible via water, known as Swim Coots. The more I read about the boat trips, the more excited I became as it would be a return to the roots of my interest in birdwatching – Grandad, a broad and a boat.

I picked him up on the day and we headed off into deepest East Norfolk. I was still at the very early stages of my recovery journey but clarity was unravelling, slowly and purposefully. We travelled on straight roads, carved through the wetlands – soft, green and boggy. All around us lay the flatlands – open, bare and wild. Looking out from the car, the grazing marshes were littered with the remnants of Norfolk's heritage: ancient ditches and hedgerows, dilapidated farm buildings and the stumpy remains of uncapped drainage mills. Following a classic ploughman's lunch at a nearby pub, we parked the car at Hickling Broad, picked up a reserve map from the visitor centre and headed out on to the boardwalk that lay in front of us, snaking its way through a bed of scrubby shrubs.

Our path was broken by the occasional spindly tree – the perfect posts for singing male birds. In one such tree sat a bird, which even at a distance I could see bore a distinct white supercilium – or eye-stripe. We both took a closer look with our binoculars. It was peachy-buff underneath and its woody upper parts were a mixture of chestnut and mahogany, reminiscent of a chocolate digestive biscuit. With the summer sun accentuating all the colour tones, it looked gorgeous. Opening its mouth and revealing a wide pink gape, it reeled off several repetitive rattling and clicking phrases. A sedge warbler, we both agreed.

As we awaited our boat trip we sat in one of the hides, watching shelducks and lapwings tend to their young. Minimal words were uttered – at times like this, they simply aren't needed. Soon we met our comrades at the jetty and departed across the broad; the reeds were now taller than us, creating a close sense of safety. A dark arc loped out of the reeds and passed over the boat, creating the most unforgettable view of a marsh harrier in flight I've ever had to this day. Everyone watched, awestruck, as it disappeared into the reeds again. These reeds, the warden told us, were where the famed Norfolk naturalist Emma Turner had camped to photograph young bitterns. He spoke of the reserve's long-standing relationship with the Cadbury family and about its boating heritage. This wasn't just a wildlife sanctuary; the whole place was an artefact.

On approaching Swim Coots, the boat slowed and we motored down a narrow dyke, with reed curtains drawn on either side. These funnelled us down towards a wooden jetty, beyond which a squat and thatched bird hide stood. As we made to alight, an all-white and very prehistoric-looking bird flew past us, low, over the reed tops. 'That's a great white egret,' stated the warden, calmly.

I was exhilarated, for this was a rare bird, so I asked him, 'Aren't they rare?'

'It's been around for a few weeks now,' he replied.

Magical.

A shunt of the hide door released the musty scent of sunbathed wood and thatch. It was dark inside, until the wooden flaps creaked open and each visitor invited sunlight in to fill the small space. Another large white bird – an egret? No. A strange creature, with a long spatulate bill, one leg cocked like a snowy flamingo. I asked the warden, 'What's that?' and gestured towards it. A cursory glance through his binoculars and he told me it was a spoonbill. Wait, another rare bird? I rustled through the pages of my pocket bird book and there it was: *Platalea leucorodia*, the spoonbill.

In the meantime, the warden had set up a spotting scope he must have had stowed away on the boat. 'Have a closer look,' he said, gesturing me over. Of course I obliged, grasping the opportunity to inspect this odd bird in closer detail. A flash of yellow dirtied its underparts and a fine crest adorned its head – just as the book described. Perfect. There were more birds too, wading birds, or waders for short, that the warden helped me to put names to – ruff, dunlin and black-tailed godwit.

We boarded our craft and moved on towards our next stopping point. Again, we channelled into a small dyke, which led on to the grassy bank that became our next mooring. As we alighted, three large brown dragonflies buzzed around our heads – hovering, inspecting us and then moving on. I asked the warden what they were and he informed me that they were Norfolk hawkers. Hawking they certainly were – a wonderfully descriptive avian term, which the *Oxford English Dictionary* defines as 'a bird or a dragonfly hunting on the wing for food'.[1] A behaviour easily observed in the presence of these draconiform beasts.

The hawkers were hawking along the edge of a woodland, into which the warden was about to lead us. Ahead of us stood the edifice of the viewing tower we were about to climb, a tall cuboid structure, moulded from steel and clad by staircases on its outer edges. Following a trudging climb, the stairs terminated at the tower apex

– a rectangular viewing platform. The view of the broads that we found up there was sensational and can only be rivalled by the panoramas found at the top of Norfolk's finest church towers, such as Ranworth.

We were spoilt. The view was sumptuous, and the reserve was spread out below us like a green and blue patchwork quilt. To the north and east ran the coastline and the iconic red and white candy stripes of Happisburgh Lighthouse could also be seen due north. The great tower of Winterton church stood to the east, and out west lay Barton Broad, the second largest of the broads. Spinning round to the south, you could see the conurbation of Potter Heigham, clustered along the side of the River Thurne – an odd place, reminiscent of a Norfolk coastal resort, but inland. We breathed the scene in and exhaled its glory.

Eventually we walked back down the tower and re-embarked our vessel for the return journey, over the water. We could have gone back to the car at this point, but we both opted to continue our walk around the reserve. Perpendicular pathways led us round the main reed bed, which sat still and sun-dried. The dusty paths guided us to another stop-off point, a small bird hide overlooking an open expanse of fenland. A sign next to the door declared it the 'Bittern Hide'. A fleeting dream passed through my mind – imagine seeing one. It was just us inside the hide and although we were treated to the wonderful sight of a distant marsh harrier, there were no bitterns present in the boggy area in front of us. This didn't spoil our day though and we were upbeat as we began the walk back towards the visitor centre and car park beyond.

'Look, Joe,' Pops exclaimed, pointing. I followed the direction of his finger, and what was this avian apparition that had appeared before us? An awkward, barrel-chested bird careered over the reeds to our right, straight over the path and then down into the main reed bed on the other side. It looked like a streaky-brown heron and I knew it was a bittern, my first ever sighting of one. *The Birds of Norfolk*[2] is a weighty tome, and features several pages dedicated to bitterns. It states that in Britain they are confined to a few breeding localities, several of which are in Norfolk. In avian terms, I feel that nothing else epitomises Norfolk like a bittern.

To share such profound experiences that day was, in simple terms, amazing. I remember the extraordinary sense of calm I felt, as if it were yesterday, a feeling that was nurtured, and grew throughout the day. A void began refilling after lying empty for a long time. I began to feel alive again.

Not only did it bring such positivity but it also brought a great sense of meaning, as if I'd found my true calling. These were all feelings that I wanted to experience again. To see more and to open my mind to the world of nature that was, itself, opening around me. That day lingers long in my memory and will linger forever. It was the start of a new interest in birdwatching and the start of my Bird Therapy – the next chapter of my life.

II.

A survey, a definition and the
five ways to well-birding

t was in 2014 that I began to take more of an interest in birdwatching as a hobby and I had also started to recognise just how positive I felt when I was immersed in the world of birds. My worries seemed to fade into insignificance and when I was feeling stressed, if I counteracted it with some time outside, watching them, it drifted off like birds do, in a stiff breeze. I became aware of some relief from certain symptoms – low mood and lack of motivation – and noted elation and what I would describe as 'ultra-positivity'. Quite simply, I started to feel a lot better.

As my interest grew, people would ask me: why? Why birdwatching? This would usually arise at the end of a conversation where I'd been ribbed for being a 'twitcher' or a 'weirdo'. I developed a generic response. Something along the lines of, 'I really enjoy it and firmly believe in its therapeutic value.' Sure, I believed what I was saying, but in truth, I hadn't put much thought into the deeper meaning of my words. Was it actually therapeutic? I pondered away at this sentiment, until one day, whilst lingering at one of these junctures of thought, I decided that the experience of birdwatching in a therapeutic sense couldn't possibly just be my own perception.

So, at the start of 2015, I decided to proverbially 'spread my wings' and find out if anybody else felt the same way about birdwatching. There'd been a few other birdwatchers I'd come across in passing who had been willing to chat to me about their own experiences, and this made me aware of a shared feeling – a spark of sorts. I wanted to reach out further and see if there was a wider network of people out there who concurred with me. These early forays and observations were the sowing of the seed that has now blossomed to an ongoing exploration into the therapeutic benefits of birdwatching for mental health and wellbeing, which I decided to name Bird Therapy.

I promise that this will be the only part of the book where I really focus on data and crunching numbers, so please bear with it. As well as the absolute wealth of research out there, I also wanted to collect some information myself. To achieve this, I made an online survey and linked it to a blog, which I'd tentatively started writing in January 2015. Half of the survey was focused on birdwatching and the other half on mental health. I ended up with 298 usable responses, which supported my research and ideas.

I was hasty though, and perhaps with support and guidance it could've been a more worthwhile piece of research, at least with regards to statistical analysis. That said, the information that people shared with me was so extensive that it consolidated my ideas about the wider benefits of birdwatching and of nature in general. Whenever I've referred to the collective data from the survey, I've stated that it's from 'survey respondents' and mostly it's been taken from a random 100; otherwise it's from the entire 298 responses. The survey questions are included at the end of the reference list at the back of the book.

I keep talking about it, but what actually is mental health? UK mental health charity Mind defines good mental health as 'being generally able to think, feel and react in the ways that you need and want to live your life'.[1] This is an excellent and succinct definition, with 'bad' mental health being the polar opposite: a cloud of irrationality, darkening and subduing everything. When I define it to my teenage students (I'm a teacher), I usually say that it's a bit of a triangle, where each side impacts on the other and vice-versa. I label the three sides as social, emotional and physical (health) and then place the term 'mental' in the centre of the triangle.

Mind provide some stark statistics about mental health in the UK with the most common and also most recognised mental health problems, anxiety and depression, affecting 5.9 and 3.3 people in every 100. From the same data set it's worth noting that 7.8 people in every 100 report a combination of both anxiety and depression. PTSD at 4.4 is also a prevalent condition, and the next most common are phobias (2.4), OCD (1.3) and panic disorder (0.6).[2]

As the survey was geared towards mental health, it's difficult to relate it to these statistics. Two hundred respondents identified as having a diagnosed mental health condition. Depression and anxiety were the most common conditions in the survey, with 145 and 97 people respectively identifying as having a diagnosis. Perhaps most interesting here was the crossover between these two conditions: 68 people identified as having a diagnosis of both depression and anxiety. Over half of all respondents with a diagnosed condition (102) had one diagnosis, with a further 81 specifying two diagnoses and the remaining 17, three or more.

As well as creating the survey, one of the first things I did when I started writing was to consider the perceived benefits that the outdoors might be able to bring to those suffering with their mental health. This seemed to be a logical starting point and most Internet searches kept turning up a term which I'd not heard before – ecotherapy. Mind had coined it, stating that it describes a range of regular and structured activities that take place outdoors and are beneficial to wellbeing.[3] I became instantly aware that birdwatching – at least how I regarded it – was a form of ecotherapy.

Reflecting on the effectiveness of ecotherapy, Kevin Fenton of Public Health England stated that, 'Many people working to improve public health will be familiar with the five ways to wellbeing. It's reassuring to see how an ecotherapy approach enables people to meet all five of these evidence-based actions.'[4] The concept of the five ways to wellbeing was one I'd encountered before, when I first started exploring my own mental health issues – and I was well aware of what a brilliant framework it is. However, I wasn't quite prepared for how well it would align with my newfound interest in birdwatching.

The five ways to wellbeing were developed by the New Economics Foundation (NEF) and endorsed by Mind. They were born from a government Foresight project that set out to investigate and project the future wellbeing of the British population. The findings were highly quantitative and the NEF were asked to dilute them for mainstream communication – hence the five ways to wellbeing were created. They are: to connect, to take notice, to give, to keep learning and to be active. I challenge any birdwatcher to look at these five areas and not recognise how wonderfully they overlay and intertwine with our hobby.

The more I considered all of these crossovers and correlations, the more that I realised how the five ways to wellbeing would make an excellent foundation for a book. A moment of clarity led to me transferring the moniker of the five ways to wellbeing into my own 'five ways to well-birding'; each providing me with a basic framework to write around and ultimately leading me to new ideas and topic areas to explore. Throughout this book, I'll explore their application and relevance to the hobby of birdwatching, recalling my own experiences and those of other people, while supplementing all of this with further research.

These collective strands draw together and present a compelling case for the therapeutic benefits of birdwatching. It's important at this stage to outline the overarching aim of this book. I am not a therapist. I am not a professor. This isn't a scientific study and I don't claim to be able to prove anything in that sense. However, I've been immensely privileged in the way that people have been willing to share their – often darkest – thoughts with me, solely because they feel as strongly as I do that birdwatching has helped them.

You'll read quotes, anecdotes, observations and ideas. There will be some dark moments and then some filled with light – and many filled to the brim with birds. You'll be introduced to existing research and to some of the profound words that people have shared with me. You'll share my experiences and we'll walk down to the lake at my patch in winter, and out on to the heath in spring.

Most importantly, I hope that you'll recognise how birdwatching has helped me and how it could possibly help you. To advocate this, each chapter ends with some practical tips to take away and apply to your own birdwatching and nature experiences. The way that birdwatching has become my main source of therapy is documented thoroughly and of all the therapies I've tried – prescribed, holistic and alternative – nothing has had the prolonged and positive impact that birdwatching has. It's time to continue with the journey.

III.

A dunnock, a Pallas's warbler and a multitude of patterns

'It has long been an axiom of mine that the little things are infinitely the most important' – Arthur Conan Doyle

Do you ever properly take notice of birds? If you do, then I wonder what the first bird was that you really took notice of. You might recall a childhood experience, you might recall something that happened not long ago. I recall the simple fact that I only took notice relatively recently, just two years before putting pen to paper.

The first bird that I really took notice of was a dunnock. A garden visitor that's often misidentified as a house sparrow and subsequently finds itself being overlooked, dunnocks are everywhere, yet we never seem to truly notice them. Where did my epiphany happen? Well, I was seated in a suburban Norwich garden on a chilly January morning, back in 2015. It wasn't quite cold enough to ice over the pond and so I heard the gentle accompaniment of trickling water as it tumbled down the ornamental waterfall.

Stationed opposite the bare hedge, notepad in gloved hands, I sat, staring at the bird feeders in anticipation. Why? I was participating in the Royal Society for the Protection of Birds' (RSPB) 'Big Garden Birdwatch'. Observing and recording the bird species seen in the garden over a designated hour, then submitting the data, so that trends can be monitored. Anyone with an interest in wildlife can join in with this easily accessible activity, and giving something back to nature can be a genuinely rewarding act.

The dunnock hopped along the edge of the naked flowerbed and joined me on the lawn, close to my freezing toes. Positioned opposite the feeders, I was patiently waiting, dreaming of goldfinches popping on to them – or perhaps even a cotton-wool-coated long-tailed tit. Instead, I was treated to nothing of the sort and so I began to watch the dunnock. It was confident alright – always a metre or so in front of me, patrolling the lawn then stopping and cocking its head to pick insects up. Occasionally it would stop and look at me and I would duly look back. I'd started to take notice.

Dunnocks are the archetypal 'little brown job', which is a term that birdwatchers tend to assign to any small, nondescript and (obviously) brown bird. If you take your time and study one properly, you'll actually see a deep palette of colours and markings taking shape. Delve further into their detail and you'll begin to realise just how intricately marked they are. Bird identification guides often remark on their 'drab brown colouring' and 'overall dark appearance'. This is a somewhat lazy conclusion, neglecting to mention the linear streaking that runs down their mantle, bold and uniform, dropping down from their smoky grey, almost blue chest and throat. These birds are subtly beautiful and not drab at all. I only discovered this because I took notice.

A pair of dunnocks are a regular feature underneath the bird feeders in my back garden. I'm sure they visit many gardens and urban green spaces, but I'm also sure that many people wouldn't recognise one at first, even third, glance. Every day, birds that are defined as common are overlooked. However, as you immerse yourself in the world of birdwatching, you come to appreciate the beauty in the common species as well as the scarcer ones. The dunnock is a prime example but, arguably, all of our garden birds fall into this category.

Garden bird feeding is by far the easiest and most accessible way to engage with birdwatching. The best thing about it is that it can take place from within the comfort of your home. I've been spending more time lately observing the birds that visit my garden feeders, with the majority of my observations from the kitchen. Our bird feeders are strategically placed so they can be viewed from all of the rear-facing windows of the house. I'm usually occupied with a culinary task, but as soon as a bird pops on to the feeder I become distracted from what I'm doing and take note of who has come to visit.

Through these observations I've been able to deduce who the regular visitors to the garden are. Like 'Colin' the coal tit, who heralds his arrival with a couple of piping '*tweee*' calls, zipping into view with a flash of wing-bars, before deftly taking a sunflower seed over to the fence for dismantling. There's also the pair of collared doves, one usually on the fence watching, as the other searches for any scraps of food left on the grass. On colder days, I know that the visitors are likely to be more varied.

These frequent guests generate a sense of consistency and safety within – two words that were recurrent in my counselling sessions. It's reassuring to know that the garden birds are there, even when I'm not, and through careful observation and the two-way relationship of feeding and watching, my garden birds have become an integral part of my life. Winter is the best time to keep an eye out, as the colder weather and reduced food availability can bring some interesting visitors to bird feeders. It's a simple pleasure, but knowing that in the depths of a cold snap I might have a troupe of long-tailed tits hanging off my feeders helps to brighten the darkest days.

In ways like this, nature and birdwatching can offer us a great deal of stability. In the life of someone living with daily mental health issues these consistencies can act as an anchor to the present and provide grounding. Take time to notice the simple pleasures around you, especially when it comes to your garden bird community. Welcome the brazen blackbird as he cocks his head on your lawn, searching for worms. Embrace the characterful robin, singing from every available song post and shadowing you as you turn over your flowerbeds. Take notice.

The garden is an excellent place to start taking notice of the bird life around you and is a perfect first step towards getting to know your bird community. The next logical progression into birdwatching is to start looking outwards and in late 2014 I began to explore my local area. I was hoping to find out more about the avifauna closer to home and to perhaps find myself a local patch; my own little slice of the natural surroundings. This is something that I'll explore the benefits of later in this book.

In seeking out localised birdwatching sites, I found myself rekindling a childhood interest in maps and geography. This then combined with a newfound interest in bird habitats and suddenly, I was interested in any cluster on a map that might appeal to the local avifauna. To develop an awareness of possible birdwatching locations, I investigated the vicinity, researching past bird sightings and learning about biodiversity. Sundays became my 'birdwatching day' and as winter was approaching, a circular driving route began to form that took in as many varied sites as possible – creating a further sense of reassurance, familiarity and comfort.

On the first of these circuits, whilst travelling between two new sites, a flurry of colour flew across the road just ahead of my car. Slowing the second gear trundle to a halt, I raised my binoculars and there sat *three* pairs of bullfinches in the bare hedge. Handbrake on, I sat, watching and breathing, slow and mindful. Bullfinches are beautiful birds. The males wear resplendent shades of salmon pink, with slate-grey shoulders and pitch-black wings and caps. Females are a little subtler, with more of a peachy-grey wash. They brought with them such brightness in those dark winter months. They resonated against their spindly hawthorn backdrop. They resonated in my mind.

Driving down another nearby lane I could see that the hedgerow was heaving with birds. Unfortunately, the hum of the engine flushed them all into flight and down on to an adjacent field. Pulling the car over to have a proper look, I alighted and sidled over to the field edge for a better view. Fifteen yellowhammers were perched in a bare tree with a single Neapolitan-ice-cream-coloured brambling amongst them. Other vibrant finches flanked them – green, gold and chaff. All are 'farmland specialists', and my focused planning to pass through some arable land had clearly paid off.

In that moment, watching the flock of finches, I was allowing myself to become lost and absorbed in the sights in front of me. In these early days of my interest in birdwatching, I was still burdened by an inability to manage and regulate my mental health. Birdwatching quickly became my escape route and I started to notice that when I was out, on my own, experiencing nature and birds in a personal and intimate way, I was more relaxed than I'd ever been before. My breathing rate slowed and I closed my mind to repetitive thoughts and worries. My only focus was observing birds and learning about them. I was losing myself in birds, in a positive way.

The notion of feeling lost has been a recurring theme throughout my life and one that kept cropping up throughout a year of weekly counselling sessions. After a few sessions discussing it, I was able to attribute it to several circumstances surrounding my childhood, which had followed me into adulthood. When faced with change, my default response is to obsessively plan everything. I named this meticulous planning and attention to detail 'mapping', in the sense that I am always trying to map my life in an effort to reduce my anxieties. Paradoxically, this leads to me having unrealistic expectations, ultimately causing more anxiety as I obsess about everything being perfect.

This process of mapping is a particularly frustrating element of my OCD and means that I constantly seek perfection. In some ways, this is quite sad, as I'm aware that I'll probably never be truly content, but what is even more frustrating is that I know, rationally, that there isn't always a perfect outcome in life, so I fall back on the things that are familiar to me. These default responses and reactions mean that when I find things unfamiliar and challenging, I can crumble under the pressure and my anxiety levels go through the roof.

This usually manifests as an emotional shutdown, during which I rapidly become embittered and defensive. Birdwatching has been a vital escape during these times, and prior to taking it up as an interest, I counteracted my negativity with compulsions and behaviours. I've been able to channel these obsessions into the hobby instead, removing some emphasis from everyday life and helping my cyclic behaviour to manifest less in other aspects of my life, such as my job.

At first, I connected this to the listing aspect of birdwatching, where one keeps lists of bird species they see. These lists can be for anywhere or anything: the garden, a particular site, over a specific time frame; you name it, a birdwatcher probably has a list for it. A list is a record. A list is continuity, order and arrangement. Lists are patterns and I absolutely love patterns. I find them rhythmic and soothing for my fizzy head. Birdwatching is awash with these logical sequences, offering a perfect and naturally occurring antithesis to the chaos of everyday life.

In paying attention to these finer details, I noticed that I was finding out more about myself. The calmness I was experiencing was going home and going to work with me. I was starting to feel more relaxed with life in general and had found the right place and time to unpack my worries. A pattern was emerging. The logic and consistency of birds makes complete sense to me; they represent freedom, in their ability to fly and escape. Several survey respondents echoed that nature made sense to them too.

Another one manifested in the way that birds appeared in particular places and at specific times. This framing of events chronologically is part of nature's own calendar, and for a novice birdwatcher, the impact of seasonal changes and weather on birds can be a daunting topic. However, exploring the depths of these rhythms can actually be comforting in itself. It fosters an understanding of how our environment alters around us and how the future arrival of migrant birds can help us look forward to our future. The first wheatears of spring arriving on the Norfolk coast act as a marker that warmer times are coming. They're nature's way of signposting us. They're nature's beacons of hope.

The pattern and repetition of visiting the same place also brought me additional balance and stability. It enabled the developing of a sense of what should, and could, turn up there. This then helped me to develop a further sense of normality and security, helping to alleviate feelings of anxiety and disappointment. As patterns help to ease my own anxiety, finding that they were firmly entrenched in my new hobby made me feel an even closer affinity with it.

From two years of attentive observation and taking notice of the patterns around me, I can tell you what to expect at my patch at most times of the year. I can tell you what to expect when the wind changes or the sun blazes. I've watched the same species come and go and their numbers rise and fall. I've seen them build nests and incubate, raise and fledge their young. I've watched them congregate in the centre of the lake when the temperature drops and take to the air in a cacophony of splashes and wingbeats when a dog-walker passes.

Visual experiences and aesthetics are also important and form the basis of much of my observation. I absolutely love the colours I discover in nature. It was August at my patch and the late summer sun was blazing down, warming my exposed arms as T-shirt weather took hold. Arriving at the usual vantage point in the south-east corner of the lake, out came the tripod's legs, as my scope took its usual position by the two alder trees. The air hung still and warm, perhaps a little heavy, like a storm was approaching.

Absorbing the panoramic view with the naked eye, I took stock of my surroundings. I was staring into a landscape painting, spellbound by every brushstroke on the canvas. The colours were so sharp and vivid in the midday sun that they all seemed to blend into one palette.

The lime and mint-green sundae shades of vegetation met starkly with the midnight-black water surface, which itself would be intermittently lit up by sunlight, transforming it into glass and revealing the caramel lake bed below. An upward glance and the light floral shades grew darker and stronger, as ancient deciduous trees rose from the lakeside. Eventually they peaked, forming an undulating border with the azure sky – no clouds could be seen.

There are so many colours and flavours to be found in natural settings – embrace and enjoy them. Next time you're outdoors, stop and immerse yourself in the colours around you. Take notice of them fully and allow them to wash over you. This primal pleasure can be easily forgotten and can be a calming and rejuvenating experience. Meditation on nature's colours is often inspirational and every outdoor space holds natural beauty.

When writing about such beauty, it can sometimes be frustratingly difficult to find the best language possible to help you, the reader, to really feel an experience for yourself and conjure up your own, matching imagery. I have to place myself back in the moment to seek out those words, and in doing so, I realise just what a blessing nature is. In a lyrical snapshot, it's incredibly hard to capture the feelings that these moments evoke. It's said that 'a picture paints a thousand words', yet I don't even think a thousand words could truly capture some pictures.

Later, I consider whether certain aspects of our environment, such as its aesthetics, can help to restore and rejuvenate us; but there's an aspect of that research that's relevant here. In his fantastic report for the RSPB, titled 'Natural Thinking',[1] Dr William Bird brought together a number of theories relating to nature and its positive effects on mental health. One of the theories he describes is called Attention Restoration Theory (ART), an idea first outlined in the 1980s by psychologists Stephen and Rachel Kaplan and one which I discovered held an obvious correlation with birdwatching.

ART identifies two forms of attention: direct and indirect. Direct attention is identified as the act of paying attention in a way that's intentional and purposeful. Conversely, indirect attention is instinctive, involuntary and natural, referred to throughout the report as 'fascination'. An example of an everyday act that fits both criteria is driving a car. Attention must be directed to the road, other road users and hazards. However, the physical act of driving, of using the pedals and changing the gears, becomes a natural process over time, something that we do without thinking – an indirect action.

Generally, indirect attention is a pleasurable act and requires little or no effort. Unlike direct attention, which actually requires us to try and can be laborious, focused more on having to do something than wanting to. This means that we have to make a concerted effort to block out any pleasurable distractions, using even more grey matter to do so. The whole process can bring about tiredness and the Kaplans coined the phrase 'directed attention fatigue' (DAF) to acknowledge this. Invariably, we'll need to have a break or rest after any spurt of directed attention, so that we can re-energise and refocus.

When applied to birdwatching, the majority, if not all, of the time spent observing birds is pleasurable. You choose to do it, but it isn't a forced action. Therefore, birdwatching could be considered as a form of indirect attention, and once I recognised this in my own birdwatching experiences, I found so much more joy in just 'being', instead of trying. The fundamental action of birdwatching – 'find bird, observe bird' – isn't tiring in itself. Obviously trudging around miles of coastal shingle, checking every inch of sea buckthorn in search of autumn migrants, is hugely tiring – but it's a direct choice to do so.

As is the 'listing' approach to birdwatching, explored more thoroughly later, but worthy of a mention here. This approach is focused on collecting something, namely 'ticks' of new birds on a list. It requires directed attention as well as a steely determination, especially when listing competitively. There are even some competitive bird-listers who will drop everything and not hesitate to travel the length and breadth of the country to add a new bird to their list – something that most would identify as the act of 'twitching'. Surely this commitment must cause a great deal of DAF in some people, thus negatively impacting on their wellbeing? Unfortunately, no competitive 'listers' responded when I tried to find out.

When you physically raise your binoculars to observe a bird, a particular conundrum arises. To observe something through your binoculars is a forced act. The binoculars have to be held up to your eyes and your attention is directed to the target. This is a bit of a paradox – although your attention is directed at the target, it's still not directed attention. Yes, it's intentional and purposeful, but it isn't laborious or tiring. Perhaps this is why I and many others find birdwatching to be such a relaxing and reinvigorating pastime. Fundamentally, birdwatching isn't a mentally strenuous activity.

In my survey, someone wrote that, 'Everything else is blocked out as you scan through a flock of waders.' What a lovely statement and thought, of scanning through a flock of birds to find your troubles dissipating. When your line of vision is cocooned by your binocular barrels, the distractions of the outside world are shut out. The only object of attention is whatever is encased within those lenses and everything else, lingering in the periphery, fades away. The mind can wander and relax, whilst still in the security of a visual and mental cushion. It allows you to disappear into an insular world – the world of birds through an optical lens.

This idea is resonant with that of 'flow', a subjective state that was identified by the Hungarian-American psychologist Mihaly Csikszentmihalyi, through various studies and observations.[2] Flow was described by his respondents as a 'current that carried them along effortlessly' – exactly how I feel when I'm outside and embracing my senses. When in a state of flow, it's felt that you can become so involved in something that you detach from time, fatigue and everything but the activity itself. It's also described as a 'merging of action and awareness', which is a lovely way of describing birdwatching too – especially when it transcends on to a more emotional or spiritual level.

As you become more confident in your avian and outdoor awareness, an additional sense starts developing. A birdwatching sense, which is obvious in those who have spent many hours observing birds and immersed in particular habitats. It's an acute awareness of any slight movement seen in vegetation, however deep or dense. I find that I can stop anywhere, allow my senses to sharpen and my breathing to slow, until I fall into an almost meditative state. I begin to detect movement and as I scan, either with binoculars or the naked eye, I start to pick up these kinetic nuances in all areas of my peripheral vision.

Focusing on any flurry of movement, a new challenge awaits me every time I choose to accept it – the challenge to identify the bird species. This may involve lengthy observations, note-taking and even taking a photograph if possible. It's a multi-faceted and multi-sensory experience that takes me away from any external worries. This challenge – this skill – can be honed on a smaller scale, perhaps at home, or in a park, garden or outdoor space. Just watching the foliage of any trees or shrubs that are familiar to you can be a fantastic baseline for developing this sense of movement. Through practice, this can be transferred to a controlled environment such as a wildlife reserve, before unleashing your newfound bird sense wherever you go.

A perfect example of this sense in action comes from a memorable day I shared with a birdwatching friend, at one of my favourite places along the Norfolk coast – Waxham. This particular friend and I share a strong affiliation with the east coast of Norfolk. I visited the area a lot as a child and as an adult; and more importantly, as a birdwatcher, I often visited in favourable conditions to try and find rare birds. Exactly what we were hoping to achieve that day.

We'd worked hard and walked far but were approaching the realisation that maybe it wasn't to be our day. After walking nearly five miles along the newly cut dune paths and back, it had begun to feel as though we weren't going to find anything particularly scarce. Although, to be fair, we'd encountered a handful of beautiful yellow-browed warblers – stunning Siberian vagrants that arrive on our shores in good numbers in late autumn. These diminutive green warblers are distinguished by the distinctive yellow eyebrow that their name suggests. This meant that the day wasn't completely devoid of the marvels of bird migration, but I could sense my friend's despondency. So, as we continued walking back down the path, I tried to invigorate him, saying, 'It will be in the next bush, mate.' Admittedly, I wasn't overly sure about this myself.

We approached an expansive beech tree, which, since the paths had been cut through the scrub, now loomed over us. Last autumn I'd had to view this area from the dune ridge above and it was great to be able to look up into the canopy from the new path. The tree was swarming with goldcrests – the smallest breeding bird in the UK, whose numbers swell on the coast in late autumn, bolstered by migrating birds from Siberia. Although tiny, they're easily recognised by the vivid golden-yellow crest on their heads. There were so many of them in that beech that I wouldn't even like to estimate their numbers, and we stopped for a while to absorb the spectacle and scan through the flock, hoping for another yellow-browed warbler to appear. Then a flicker of movement directly in front of me caught my attention.

It was the combination of movement and lurid colour that had drawn my eye, a flash of yellow below the darkened overhang of the tree. I'd been studying my bird books to get to know which Siberian wanderers we might encounter that day. The brightness of the yellow – could it be a Pallas's leaf warbler? I called to my friend: 'Pallas's?!' A moment, a heartbeat – I waited. He quickly trained his binoculars over to where I was looking and soon we were both observing the bird in question. Flitting through the branches was a stunning little bird, a combination of greens and yellows; a lemony rump, bright double wing-bars and a bulbous central crown stripe. This is a key feature of Pallas's leaf warblers – bold, prominent and the colour of warm custard. 'Yes, it is,' he replied.

It was only because of that initial movement that we even saw this magnificent bird. My bird sense had definitely worked. It was the first time I'd seen one of these Siberian sprites and it filled me with a great feeling of joy and a real sense of camaraderie to have found it with a birdwatching friend. Not only was this a new bird for me but I'd also been building myself up to potentially seeing one, drilling the description into my mind. That made it feel even more special and what had seemed like a damp squib of a day was now charged with an electric, positive energy.

This is all part of the waiting game that birds often play with you. You have to counter them by honing your innate ability to notice the subtle motions in nature. Waiting. Breathing. Knowing that a skulking bird is behind that foliage, or hearing a snatch of birdsong and patiently preparing for the singer to appear. This game of hide and seek can be invigorating – especially if you're using all your senses to locate a bird. It requires patience, where mindfulness approaches such as slow breathing and immersive observation can be helpful, ultimately promoting relaxation and calm.

I believe that the more I've taken notice of and absorbed the natural world around me, the more self-aware I've become. I contemplate things, I relax, I inhale and I take notice. This has helped me also to recognise when I'm stressed or my mood is low and to become more aware of myself and my interactions with the world around me. Overleaf I share with you some tips on how to bring the ethos of noticing into your birdwatching and wider outdoor experiences.

A few practical tips about taking notice of birds

Get to know the birds in your garden or any nearby outdoor space and notice how they behave and interact.

Try to develop a sense of 'being' whilst birdwatching, rather than overtly trying.

Take time to notice the intricacies of feather patterns and markings. Some of the most beautiful, underrated birds are around us every day.

Pay attention to how being outside and engaging with birds makes you feel. Harness positive experiences and try to recognise what makes them so.

Reflect on and absorb the colours in nature and in outdoor settings. Try to appreciate them more everywhere.

Develop your 'bird sense' – it can reveal so many of nature's secrets to you.

IV.

A pipit, a woodlark and an evening concerto

'Those little nimble musicians of the air, that warble forth their curious ditties' – Izaak Walton

When you work with young people defined as challenging, you naturally come to expect that you'll be challenged. This is a daily occurrence in my field of work, as a teacher of young people who've been excluded from school, all of whom have some degree of special educational need. A thick skin is a requisite for such roles and is necessary for repelling the profane attacks and criticisms that are regularly aimed at you. When you've spent many hours planning lessons and making resources, being persistently told that your lessons are 'shit', as is your teaching, can stretch your resilience to new limits. This is a given, even a daily expectation, but it eventually takes its toll.

At a particularly bad time, a lack of support coupled with a poorly managed work/life balance had led to anxious feelings, starting from the moment I woke up and lasting all day, every day. My mind would tick and whirr long into the evenings, skittling over into my sleep. Once this mindset takes hold, my ability to cope diminishes, my mood drops and I find my motivation drifting away, until flatness prevails. I become crippled by paranoid anxiety. A pressure in my brain, nagging and questioning and fuelling an underlying belief that I've done something wrong. That I've failed.

It was a day of few students, four in fact, although they were four of the county's 'finest' excluded ones. We'd have such wonderful days with them, my colleague and I, running projects encompassing multiple subjects and leading trips that delighted and informed. We also had days like the day I'm writing about – days when they tried all they could to break us. I don't remember the exact words and events that led to me walking out, but I can loosely recall the moment of self-implosion.

I was sitting in the faded common room on one of the donated sofas, a sad seating arrangement decorated with drab grey floral patterns that resembled dying plants. These students couldn't be trusted with smart modern embellishments; besides, the organisation couldn't afford them anyway. I sat with three of them (one had already gone home by that point), who were all flatly refusing to do anything, other than obstinately argue every attempt at reasoning.

My colleague was in the office, arranging transport and calling parents to arrange 'send homes', the idea being that we would all start afresh the next day, no grudges from either side. A flawed system perhaps, but those were the parameters we were given. I sat supervising the students, ready to diffuse any further issues – and that's when the personal attacks started. I was a 'fucking useless teacher', a 'fucking joke', I 'tried too hard' and they'd 'never change' no matter what I did. This continued for several minutes until suddenly my resilience broke. My anger and frustration at their relentless personal undermining reached boiling point and my armour buckled.

I rang my boss, who promised to come straight over and said to wait until then. I'm ashamed to say that even after getting away from the students and into the office, I couldn't cope. I was in the throes of panic – my head was bubbling and throbbing so much that I walked out, got into my car and drove off. I'd abandoned my post and left my colleague in a vulnerable position, something which I still beat myself up over to this day.

Inside the car, my head and heart were pounding. What had I done? Surely this was going to cost me my job, and potentially my career. As with all situations like this, my default is to go to the extreme, and I started thinking about the wider implications. This stoked my anxiety and I began to plan my escape and, at worst – taking my own life. As I drove, shaking, I decided that I needed to be somewhere outdoors, on my own, where I could stop and try to rationalise my thoughts. All roads were subconsciously leading to my patch and specifically the heathland portion of it. I honestly can't remember driving there though – everything was working on autopilot.

A recollection – of walking along the dry, dusty path that crosses the top edge of the heath. Wafting over the dry ground came the sweet coconut scent of flowering gorse, bathing the ochre ridge with a tropical air. Reflecting, worrying, overthinking and replaying negative thoughts over and over. Focus. Breathe. Calm down! Slowly but surely, the soothing effects of being outdoors were coming – the heath had been a wise choice. Stepping off the main path on to a more rugged one, it felt more natural and looked less trodden by the local dog-walkers. Slightly offset from the main arterial walkways, it weaved in and out of gorse and bramble. This was definitely the right route to feeling closer to nature.

All thoughts were interrupted as a small, streaky bird alighted from a nearby tree and then dropped slowly on stiff wings. It resembled an avian parachutist as it floated down and an outpouring of happy and melodious song was released, which fluted and tumbled all around the heath. A whirlpool of sound, cancelling out the cyclone of thoughts. The tempo increased until it stopped entirely, as it settled atop the same tree it had risen from. The bird was a tree pipit in the midst of its captivating song flight. Scarce for the heath although found at a few other sites in Norfolk.

Regardless of my wretched frame of mind, this delightfully descending ditty brought a smile back to my face and briefly erased what had led me to be there in the first place. It was a sound so sweet that it seemed to carry light into a dark moment. It was nature's torchbearer. I found myself in a place so serene and calming that, when coupled with such melody, it became a comfort blanket of sorts. On that day, the combination of birdsong and being outdoors had helped to alleviate acute symptoms of stress and anxiety. Birdsong. I hadn't considered how powerful it could be.

A recent study by King's College, London, found that birdsong can boost mental wellbeing for several hours. Volunteers were asked to record their moods on a mobile application as they moved around cities, and the researchers found that there was a tangible improvement to wellbeing following exposure to birdsong, trees and even from just seeing the sky. The positive effects, as well as being immediate, were found to be present up to four hours later.[1]

Another piece of earlier research investigated whether birdsong alone can convey restorative properties. In its summary, birdsong was the sound that participants most commonly associated with their own restorative experiences with nature. The study went on to discuss that our perception of the restorative properties of the songs of different birds can vary according to their 'acoustic, aesthetic and associative properties'.[2] For example, the harsh calls of corvids, such as carrion crows, aren't the most pleasing – being grim and guttural – with this negative view perhaps being reinforced by their wholly black appearance and perceived nastiness.

It's interesting that we attach different properties and perceptions to bird sounds and I find that we attach these sounds to places too. Whilst finalising this chapter, I found myself being periodically serenaded by the trilling staccato of a wren that had recently taken residence in the back garden. Whenever it sang, I stopped writing. I stopped and looked for it and most importantly – I smiled. It became a familiar sound, and a sound I almost came to expect. A habitual and localised melody that was anchoring me in the present. My ever-supportive garden wren.

Listen out for and become aware of the bird sounds close to you, as unwrapping these sonic layers can help you to build a stronger relationship with your garden bird community. But what about the bird sounds heard outside the perimeters of your garden or local area? Perhaps those of the coast or farmland? I really started to think about this when I was left a comment on a forum, stating that, 'Nothing chills me out like the sound of a curlew.'

The sound of a curlew is haunting and beautiful, but when had I last heard one myself? It was a few weeks prior to writing, at Blakeney Harbour in North Norfolk. Walking along these estuarine channels lined with sailing boats, the only sound was the clang of metal against mast. Then a mournful, upturned whistle came ghosting across the bleak and open landscape – 'Curl-*ew*'. A sound synonymous with the coast, and the coast itself synonymous with relaxation.

If someone asked me which bird sound signifies the coastal flats of Norfolk, it would *have* to be the curlew. It's such an evocative sound – one that instantly conjures imagery of serpentine channels, spartan salt marshes and sprouting samphire. A perfect example of how bird sounds can evoke memories; in this case, of a relationship with a specific area or habitat. If the curlew is the calling card of the coastal flats, which bird would epitomise my favourite habitat? Who would be the herald of the heathland?

We hadn't had a manager at work for some time and the stresses of picking up all the management reporting was taking its toll. It meant an awful lot of working at home, holed up in the study, putting together reams of statistical data – work/life balance, what was that? Solace came from weekend visits to the Norfolk coast to go birdwatching with a friend, but often after work a nature fix was required and so I would stop off at the heath to unwind.

During one of these stop-offs, I was standing statue-like in the middle of the heath. Standing and slowly breathing. Standing and carefully listening. Fresh aromas filled the nostrils – coconut, wood and soil. Blue tits and goldcrests busied themselves around the gorse, gathering insects for their late-afternoon feasts. Whilst acutely absorbing this sensory experience, a distraction came in the form of a small bird, sitting low in the dry ground-scrub. It was definitely a lark and a closer inspection revealed the white reverse neck-collar of a woodlark. I begged for it to soar into display flight and perhaps it heard my silent pleas, as it rushed up from the floor and high into the blue sky above.

It flew upwards until it was nothing but a distant dot. Then I heard it – no, I felt it. Filling my ears and mind and smothering the heath in wondrous song. The first time you hear a woodlark sing is a magical moment and one that's never forgotten. It's a difficult song to describe: melancholic yet vitalising, a descending staccato of piped notes that lift and swirl in a flurry of sweet melody. I was awestruck by its beauty and clarity; it was the loveliest birdsong I'd ever heard. It saturated me with joy and I left the heath a hundred times happier.

The woodlark is certainly the herald of the heathland, but who would provide the fanfare of the forest or the message of the marshland? I posed a question on social media, asking which bird sounds people connected to specific habitats and I received some evocative responses. Several people also connected curlew calls with coastal marshland, along with the piping calls of redshanks and oystercatchers. Skylarks also featured, evoking memories of childhood and farmland. One response described a robin's trill as 'nature's companionship'. Fitting that the robin's song follows us through the entire year, singing into the lightest of summer evenings and on the darkest of winter days. A true companion of nature.

Reflecting upon woodland walks in spring, two bird sounds sprung to mind as being part of the experience – the nuthatch and chiffchaff. Interestingly, someone else made the exact same connection in those social media responses. What about reed beds? That has to be the iconic boom of the bittern. A sound I didn't hear until my mid-twenties, when it reverberated out to me across the rolling reed beds of Strumpshaw Fen. It's another bird sound that's incredibly difficult to describe, recalling a foghorn or perhaps someone blowing into an empty bottle.

There are, in fact, many bird songs that are difficult to describe in writing, and none more so than that of the nightjar. I'm lucky that a small number of these odd birds spend their summers very close to where I live. So close that they reside within the boundaries of my local patch, favouring its dry, scrubby heaths. Not only are they birds of the heathlands, but they are also nocturnal, in both song and flight, spending their days camouflaged against the parched earth.

It felt close and sticky as I stepped out of the car in the failing light. The first sound that rode across the warm evening airwaves was the onomatopoeic chant of a cuckoo. From car park to clearing, the path led me onward, into what was essentially a gorse-lined tunnel. It was so narrow at times that gorse spikes scratched annoyingly at my head as I walked; but that sharpness of the gorse bushes was offset by the smooth fluidity of the cuckoo's rhythmic song.

Eventually, the gorse receded and open heathland lay sprawled out on either side, with a tree line running distantly across this shadowy vista, outlining a clear and obvious boundary. The path bowed round to the left and skirted along the edge of the trees. Walking slowly but purposefully, I arrived at a natural halt that felt like a good position to wait for the spectral fliers. Standing, waiting – I really should've brought a chair. Ambling and agitating – had I chosen the wrong evening?

Then it began.

How do you even begin to describe the ethereal singing of the nightjar to someone who has never heard it before? The first word that springs to mind is 'mechanical', especially as its pitch seems to shift up or down in gears. The 'jar' in nightjar is derived from 'churr', which is what the song is supposed to sound like. That churring was the exact sound that was reeling away behind me so I headed back towards it, closing in on a cleared area of gorse. In the semi-darkness, sitting in full view on a tree stump, looking like a broken tree branch itself, was the purveyor of the song.

Oh, to be so close to such an oddity of the avian world. To be alone, on a warm summer's evening, in the company of nothing else but nature. I spent an hour in the presence of four nightjars, who treated me to an otherworldly display of churring and wing-clapping. Darkness fell and the whirring symphony continued around me, creating a panoramic soundscape that, even though I couldn't see the birds, helped me to feel their presence. During an interval in their evening concerto, I began the long walk back to my car, feeling elated, ecstatic even. I was only a few miles from my house, yet I had been able to experience something so powerful. A privilege of nature.

The nightjar also shares its primetime slot with another bird and another that carries the word 'night' in its name. The nightingale is a migratory bird, as is the nightjar, with both spending their winters in Africa. Nightjars sing at night as it's the time when their prey – moths, beetles and other flying insects – is most active. Nightingales sing at night, well, because they can. A month after my nightjar fix, a friend told me where I could go to listen to nightingales singing locally.

It meant a slight detour on my way home from work, but having never heard one of nature's most renowned songsters before I felt it was worth it. I shared the site with another friend, who said that after a stressful day at work, nightingale song would sometimes provide them with the means to de-stress. I was hopeful that if I was lucky enough to encounter them at the local site, I might be able to test these rejuvenating effects for myself.

I tried my luck one evening, but to no avail. I thought I'd heard a few scratches of song drift past, but nothing quite tangible enough to fully acknowledge their presence, and so I decided to have another go the following day. On arrival, I noted that it was a stuffy evening, the kind that gives you a bit of a headache. It was too warm and I didn't fancy traipsing around, so I positioned myself on a picnic bench that sat next to a patch of dense scrub the size of a small bungalow. I waited for ten minutes – nothing. Twenty minutes – still nothing. This was where I'd been told to go. The best spot. Maybe it just wasn't to be.

I was beginning to feel a little despondent after my efforts – then it came. Too often, we try to attach adjectives to describe sounds and experiences, but it really is impossible with nightingale song. It's a genuinely sublime sound that bubbles and pulses – it's powerful and true. I did it then, tried to attach superlatives to something I simply can't do justice to. If I could recommend a single birdsong to experience when you're feeling low, then the song of the nightingale would be top of the list. I've been back to the same spot at the same time of the year many times. It's somewhere I know that I can go when I want to be on my own, to be wrapped up in one of the most beautiful sounds of nature. It's somewhere I can go to feel better.

In 2016, I went back to the same picnic bench and sat. There was no song this time – just gravelly snippets of subdued sub-song. I felt dispirited that I couldn't close my eyes, soak up that precious sound and recharge my emotional batteries. However, something equally enthralling happened. I found myself at eye level with a bird that I didn't recognise; drab, long-tailed, sleek and plainly beautiful. I soon realised that it was the evening soloist himself, the nightingale. I looked at him and he looked at me, croaked and then turned around, disappearing back into the foliage. It was a fleeting moment where we both just knew. Seldom seen and often heard. I smiled to myself and returned home – content.

There are others who hold the nightingale song in reverie too, the most well known being John Keats with his classic poem 'Ode to a Nightingale'. I won't deconstruct its literary worth here, but if you read it for yourself you may appreciate the intoxicating descriptions he uses to describe the feelings that hearing nightingale song can induce. In the 1920s, the BBC aired a radio broadcast that featured a cellist and a nightingale in an unlikely, but haunting, duet. It proved so popular, especially to those whose urban locales weren't frequented by such birds, that it was repeated every year for a further eleven years.

I asked on social media what people felt was the most uplifting of all birdsongs and was surprised when the nightingale wasn't chosen. Thirty-seven people responded and ten chose the blackbird. Various reasons were stated, but the general consensus was that it filled people with joy and stimulated positive memories of summer evenings. As with 'my' woodlark, we clearly do attach birdsong to certain experiences, events and feelings, particularly restorative ones.

Thinking of other times in my life when birdsong had played a profound role, I found myself reminiscing about secondary school. Deep in the shadowy catacombs of my mind, I recalled reading a piece of First World War poetry in an English class. There was a memory of skylarks. Yes – we'd studied the power of their song and how it acted as a sonic beacon of hope for those on the frontline. I looked into it again and not only did the skylark feature heavily in First World War verse but also within poetry in general. I started with the poem 'To a Skylark' by Percy Bysshe Shelley.

Shelley wrote about the beauty of the skylark's song and the emotions it aroused. He described the song sumptuously in the lines, 'Pourest thy full heart/In profuse strains of unpremeditated art.' Powerful and perfect words for describing the complex beauty of the song and its jaunty, unplanned melodies. He encapsulated the rising song flight in the lines, 'Higher still and higher/ From the earth thou springest', conjuring up a sense of the skylark's intrinsic connection to its habitat.

How I love the song of the skylark.

I remember walking out on to the heath on a bright April day. Through the wooden entrance gate, the path meanders until you're stood at an elevated vantage point. Here lies an expansive view of a somewhat alien landscape. Pockmarked and sand-scarred, the gorse contrasts starkly with the sky. Here – looking out across this rolling vista – is where they started. One by one they took flight: one, two, three and then eventually eight skylarks had taken to the air, demanding my attention as they defended their pockets of heath. Each trying to oust their neighbour as the top musician, their songs seemed to melt into a tumultuous wave, like Shelley wrote: 'singing still dost soar and soaring ever singest.'

William Wordsworth described the skylark as an 'ethereal minstrel', showing that their song has clearly been an inspiration to many people throughout history. This led me to an article entitled 'Britain's Sonic Therapy'[3] which further discussed the symbolism of skylarks in the First World War trenches. As I had studied at school, it stated that many letters home from the frontline described the solace and comfort found through birds and their songs, stating that the skylark and its cascading, energetic trilling stood for escape and for the fields of home.

This in turn then led me back to the war poetry that was the original catalyst for this reading, and I chose to rummage at the local library in the hope of finding an anthology. I was in luck, as on the pedestal of 'classic reads' sat a First World War poetry collection[4] which I duly borrowed. The word 'lark' was mentioned many times, with skylarks being specifically mentioned in two poems. One, by Isaac Rosenberg, was titled 'Returning, We Hear the Larks' and carried a positive tone, describing their singing as a joyous sound. A particular line recalled my own experiences, 'Music showering our upturned list'ning faces', as I'd stood on the heath so many times myself, under a shower of sweet music.

It became evident that I'd never truly appreciated the benefits of birdsong, for me and for others. Foolish perhaps as birds sing predominantly during the breeding season, falling roughly between February and August. These are milder times all round, stirring warm memories of the effortless transition of spring into summer. The glaring sun above, with no breeze to cool it. The stifling air punctuated by familiar sounds: the gravelly scratch of a whitethroat and the mewing of a distant common buzzard. These are good memories, arousing positive feelings. When I remember a place, it always has a backing track of birdsong – recalled distantly as if I wasn't really there, but then heard again in my mind as if I was.

I'd like to share a recent experience. It was yet another time of transition at work, fuelling my stresses and anxieties to a frenetic level. My job was altering and my teaching subject was to become mathematics. It was exciting to become a 'proper' teacher but my subjects usually being life skills and humanities, I felt weighted by the topic. This had led me to become extremely obsessive about my lesson planning and I was working at home far too much. On my way home one day, I decided, rather spontaneously, to counteract my negative thought processes with a stroll around the patch, as the evening rolled in.

It had been a fairly standard walk, with most of the resident species on show around the usual circuit. Near the car park, at the end of the walk, seemed the perfect place to stop. An outpost, looking down from the footpath on to a procession of poplar trees, bony and brush-like in the February chill. The sky was becoming increasingly dark, dissolving the last light of the day into an inky purple wash. A hubbub began to rise nearby. Blackbirds mainly, chattering away as they settled for the night – a smooth and cathartic sound that was incredibly relaxing.

It was getting darker every second and instinctively, I closed my eyes, slowed my breathing and allowed myself to be wrapped up by the duvet of sound. My worries and concerns floated away and I started to feel at one with the world. After several minutes I opened my eyes and, feeling relaxed and rejuvenated, continued the walk back to my car, smiling.

Three years after my breakdown, I was deemed to be in enough of a state of recovery to be offered a place on one of the popular eight-week mindfulness courses offered by our local wellbeing services. One of the sessions introduced us to the idea of mindfulness of sound and it became clear to me that I'd been practising mindfulness whilst birdwatching, without even realising it. I'd done it several times at my patch, stopping and sitting down on the bench that overlooks the shaded pool. Sitting there, I'd close my eyes and allow myself to fall into a meditative state.

If the day had no discernible breeze, then the only sounds came from birds. The urgent contact calls of a flock of long-tailed tits. The distant song of a mistle thrush. The urgent ticking of a robin. They're always there, so: Stop. Listen. Embrace. Absorb and enjoy. Please. I leave you with some practical tips on how to perhaps utilise and experience the therapeutic benefits of birdsong for yourself.

A few practical tips about listening to bird sounds

Familiarise yourself with the natural sounds of your bird community, either in your own garden or in a place you visit often. As you spend more time immersed in these sounds, you'll find that over time they help to anchor you to the present.

Approach the outdoors as a truly multi-sensory experience. Try not to focus on just seeing birds – try to hear them too. There is so much pleasure in identifying a bird by its call or song.

The top ten uplifting birdsongs and calls shared with me were: blackbird, curlew, skylark, nightingale, willow warbler, blackcap, wren, robin, oystercatcher and song thrush. Try and learn these and then listen out for them.

When listening to natural sounds, don't be afraid to accept the whole soundscape, rather than becoming too focused on individual bird sounds. Every sound is a passing moment, so treat them as such and enjoy them accordingly.

V.

A bittern, the binocular code and the art of finding rarities

'One touch of nature makes the whole world kin' – William Shakespeare

To maintain my wellbeing since I broke down, I had to make wholesale lifestyle changes. As well as being mentally unfit there was also an element of being physically unfit too, and the Mental Health Foundation states that the two shouldn't be as disconnected as they currently are, with clear correlations between poor mental health and long-term physical health conditions.[1] However, the biggest impact on my own overall health came from excessive alcohol consumption and this was something that had to stop.

It felt especially difficult, as my relationship with alcohol had always been on a knife-edge and practically every social relationship in my life at that time had been built around drinking. In private, I drank daily and on my own. It was an ongoing problem. A battle; and as I wound it down, over a period of six months or so, I began to see a lot less of my old circle of friends. I'd expected an organic breakdown in our relationships to occur and to begin with, quite honestly, I really struggled with it. It made me agitated and frustrated – probably because I felt the need to drink, but equally due to my lack of social interaction.

This isn't to say that I felt lonely or bored – a large part of making myself feel mentally better came from accepting who I am and enjoying my own company again. This also led to the rediscovery of my long-suppressed passion for the outdoors, starting with walking. I'd always enjoyed walking and looking at old buildings, so the first stage of my self-directed therapy was to go on walks, on my own or with my partner. We began to look forward to visiting new places and we started to make our own connections with the outdoors.

It was on one of our outdoor forays that we paid a visit to the RSPB Strumpshaw Fen Nature Reserve – a place I visited often in my youth and one which, for me, held much nostalgia. After a brisk walk around the reserve, we arrived at Tower Hide and climbed the steps to its lofty vantage point. Gently opening the door and releasing the familiar woody smell of bird hides, I saw that there were several other people sitting on the low bench in front of us.

As this was still a raw time we didn't really interact, although my partner acknowledged them with a nod as we sat down close by. The view from up in the Tower Hide is vast, like avian widescreen, and allows you to see right across the entire reed bed that the reserve is renowned for.

A carpet of light-brown reeds gently adjusting with the wind, the occasional gnarled tree or patch of wiry scrub breaking through. Houses on the distant ridge and a bustling boatyard sat distantly down the River Yare – reminders of urban normality. Roots.

As we looked out of the hide, the unmistakable and lumbering shape of a bittern appeared, flying low over the reed tops. 'Bittern,' I cried out, gesturing in its general direction and wanting to share this wonderful sighting with the others. In birdwatching, to 'connect' with a bird is to see it – intentionally or not. In that moment, we had all connected with the bittern, thus creating another connection between us in the process.

In the *Oxford English Dictionary* two of many definitions of the word 'connect' are: 'Join together so as to provide access and communication' and 'Form a relationship or feel an affinity'.[2] Just then I'd communicated in order to help others to access the delight of this bittern, and whilst it created only a brief moment of recognition between us all, it made me feel part of something. More connections were starting to form.

In the very early days of my burgeoning interest in birdwatching, all roads seemed to lead to Cley Marshes on the North Norfolk coast. This NWT reserve is renowned as a mecca for wading birds, or 'waders' as they're colloquially known; so where better to try and identify some common ones than there? A brisk stroll through a reed bed, dissected by boardwalk, led to Daukes Hide. I entered cautiously and inside sat two older gentlemen who looked every inch the archetypal birdwatcher. I felt a little uncomfortable for having disturbed them. Their drab facade of greens and browns would soon reveal the true drabness behind it.

What was the small bird on the island? The heat haze was rendering it difficult for me to focus. I heard the two gentlemen start discussing it and an opportunity arose. 'Excuse me, I was wondering if you'd be able to help me with that bird please?' They turned and scoffed before one said, in a derisory tone, that I should purchase some better birdwatching equipment, before shunning me and continuing their mutterings.

A fair but perhaps unnecessary observation. This disheartening experience almost ended my early explorations into the hobby. I realised though that I had to learn and I had to get better at birdwatching, but where should I start? As with any shared interest it is, of course, naturally beneficial to associate and engage with likeminded people, and this can forge strong pathways towards learning, participation and enjoyment. I had to connect with other birdwatchers.

My first connective mission was to find a local birdwatching group to join and use as a platform for engagement. I started with a group that was affiliated to a wider nature organisation, which seemed like the most logical starting point. It was long established and met very close to home – a phone conversation later and it was arranged for me to pop into the next meeting. How exciting, the possibility of being in the presence of other likeminded people – people with the same interest – but I was to be disappointed.

Upon arrival, the room had a musty air to it, perhaps because we were in a village hall and these establishments, especially the older ones, sometimes seem to possess a stale odour. The entire vibe in the room seemed to lack vigour and purpose; it was formulaic and perhaps even a little antiquated. The speaker at the meeting was very interesting and engaging but, overall, there wasn't a focus on birdwatching as a hobby, especially regarding social inclusion – the reason I was there.

Floating around the room in the interval and conversing with a few people led me to the group's trip leader, trips seemingly being the most sensible way to engage in some actual birdwatching. However, on approaching him for a chat, he seemed ashamed to share with me that he was lucky if two people turned up for each one. This was saddening and only served to reinforce the lack of spirit I perceived within the group.

After the disheartening experience of the two gentlemen in the bird hide, followed by the stale group vibe, the relative anonymity of the Internet beckoned. Soon I was reading a birdwatching forum that served as an online hub for topical discussion. It even had its own Norfolk forum, where I tentatively placed a few posts. Admittedly though, I rushed in with a wishful misidentification of a short-eared owl at a local site. This prompted a number of private messages that seemed to question my very integrity.

How dare I insinuate that this species was present at this time of the year; how dare I make such a mistake? This was the first time I experienced the pressure-cooker environment of *serious* birdwatching; however, these one-sided duels with the warriors of the keyboard served only to help steer me on my own course.

In the midst of this minor furore, I received two positive private messages. One from a gentleman I've now met several times whilst birdwatching, offering me encouragement in light of some of the negativity that had been aimed in my direction. The second from a birdwatcher who had deduced my age from my forum username and asked if there was 'another young birdwatcher in Norfolk?' This second, chance message was to be the start of a good friendship, and I felt like the foundations for a wider network of connections were starting to be laid.

Further research uncovered a different local group and another telephone conversation confirmed my attendance at their next meeting. Such a different vibe awaited me – the complete opposite of the first group, with genuine warmth in the room, reminiscent of a cosy hug inviting me to come in and stay. There were many years between myself and the next-youngest person in the room but it didn't feel like it mattered. This was the first experience I'd had where birdwatching visibly removed barriers, in this case mainly of age and socioeconomic status.

At this first meeting, acquaintance was made with

a local birdwatcher who resided close to me, and we arranged to meet up the following weekend. They were to be the first non-family member I would experience birdwatching with. It's interesting, then, that eight survey respondents specifically stated that they preferred to go birdwatching with likeminded people or those that shared their interest.

This shared interest can be incredibly helpful for anyone new to birdwatching – providing advice, guidance and mentorship. These first connections nurtured the development of my own knowledge base: of local sites and habitats, of bird sounds and of visual identification skills. It's definitely a fantastic starting point for any novice birdwatcher or nature enthusiast to begin broadening their interest.

Social media, another great connective platform, enabled me to reach out and enquire if there were any younger birdwatchers willing to share their experiences of birdwatching breaking down age barriers. Three people contacted me through email to share their anecdotes in greater depth, and interestingly, these three people were all female. Perhaps indicative of the stereotype that men are less willing to discuss their emotions? The key theme running through the three responses was a strong feeling that birdwatching had positively removed age barriers and all shared direct experiences to reinforce their views.

One stated that birdwatching had given her the confidence to speak to anyone, of any age, and that she felt that birdwatching connected people of all ages. Another said that she rarely came across any other local birdwatchers under the age of forty – but that none of the birdwatchers she met seemed bothered that she's in her early twenties. The final person shared a lovely anecdote where she was sitting in a hide, discussing and identifying a great white egret with a much older birdwatcher. She said that she 'couldn't think of any other situation where I'd just start casually having a chat with a man probably three times my age, but birdwatching does have that effect'.

Overall, birdwatching is a non-judgemental hobby, but as with any subculture there are politics embedded within it – although these seem more prevalent in the worlds of twitching and big listing (explored shortly). There are clear examples in the public domain that show just how judgemental and hyper-competitive these approaches to birdwatching can be. However, most of my own experiences in birdwatching have been positive. I do tend to fret over what people think about me, but birdwatching is a hobby that's centred on sharing, whether that's the sharing of a locally rare sighting or having a look through somebody else's scope to see a distant wader that you can't quite appreciate through your binoculars.

In my inaugural birdwatching days, I spent a lot of time at a local wildlife site called Sparham Pools. The pools are the by-product of years of gravel extraction and these man-made waterbodies are a typical sight throughout the Wensum Valley – with several being publicly accessible for fishing or nature recreation purposes. My aim was to build my foundation birdwatching knowledge through focusing on the commoner species first.

Sparham seemed perfect, as even though it's a small-scale reserve it holds a decent range of habitats. The main pool is encircled by a thin halo of woodland, creating a natural 'bowl' effect. The path running from the car park leads through a thin copse, before opening out on to pastel-coloured wildflower strips and luscious hedgerows. A walk at most times of the year can easily yield fifty species of bird and it's a brilliant location for honing bird identification skills.

I had an experience there that might be deemed inconsequential by many people but resonates with me to this day. It was early and was one of those mornings you can only describe as 'grey'. The sky was overcast and dampness hung heavy in the air – along with a stifling silence. On the way from the car park, the gorse is overgrown, creating a sensation of being squeezed along the path. Reaching a sharp right-hand turn, you're directed along a line of majestic oak trees, which are a summer haven for purple hairstreak butterflies. The inclination to continue walking here is strong, but there is a little detour at this corner that leads on to a field edge – the perfect place to stop and look for any feeding finches.

Not long after deviating from the path, I sensed movement along the field edge and parted some foliage to afford myself a better view. This revealed the blushed-pink tones of several chaffinches, dropping down to feed in the furrows, before flying back to the tree line in unison. I sensed further movement behind me and an elderly gentleman sidled up alongside me, accompanied by a somewhat portly black Labrador. 'What are you watching?' he asked me.

'Those chaffinches feeding there, can you see them?' I gestured in their direction and he nodded an affirmation.

This led to a conversation, in which he regaled me with tales of his garden feeders, how much he enjoyed the colours of the visiting siskins and how despondent he was that they hadn't visited that winter. He asked if I'd seen siskins before but I explained to him that I was in my birdwatching infancy and was yet to encounter them. He said that I would love them when I did and bade me farewell, his overweight hound tottering after him as they ambled back into the gorse tunnel. He left me standing with the chaffinches and contemplating the power that birds and birdwatching seemed to have for uniting people.

I realised that there needn't be any pressure associated with the natural enjoyment of birds, something that ended up being one of the principle messages underpinning Bird Therapy. A simple conversation had shown me just how accessible birdwatching could be and had reinforced the benefits of sharing an interest. A shared interest that transcends social dynamics and got me thinking. I've been visiting my private parkland patch for over three years and as a regular visitor, I've got to know some of the residents by face and name and often stop to have a chat with them.

The majority of them know what I'm doing there and the binoculars round my neck act as an unspoken code that I'm a birdwatcher.

This 'binocular code' serves as an invitation for members of the public to approach, engage and enquire. These enquiries are usually something along the lines of, 'Are you looking for something in particular?' or, 'Seen anything good?' Most birdwatchers will be able to relate to these questions, and most birdwatchers are willing to engage and share their hobby with others. You never know, them knowing that you're watching something notable in an area they're familiar with may spark their own interest. In the case of my patch, I hope it reinforces to the residents how lucky they are to live in such a species-rich location.

The binocular code comes into its own when visiting a nature reserve, and this is where the innate connections between birdwatchers are most obvious. As I trudge down boardwalks and boggy footpaths, almost every person I encounter has that familiar calling card of black or camouflage-green optical equipment somewhere about their person. Following a cursory and sometimes nervous glance, interaction tends to come fairly naturally between us. It often follows a similar template to the one in the previous paragraph. 'Seen much?'; 'Anything good about?'; or in the case of a so-called target bird, 'Have you seen it?'

A study by the Canadian Department of Natural Resources[3] looked into the motivations of birdwatchers and categorised wildlife enthusiasts into different specialisations. One of these is to be affiliation oriented, which is to engage with wildlife recreation in order to accompany or spend time with another person or people, enjoy their company and strengthen personal relationships. When I first started birdwatching I was definitely trying to connect in this way but I do accept that this was also due to the social void in my life from my lifestyle changes.

Some of the people I met in these early days became my friends as well as just birdwatching companions and I find it inspiring that a shared interest could form the foundations for friendship. From a random hundred, ten people in my survey mentioned words pertaining to friendship, friends and socialising when sharing what they felt they'd gained from birdwatching. One respondent shared a wonderful anecdote about social interactions and birdwatching, which also touched upon the general accessibility of the hobby:

> You can do it on your own or with other people, but when I do it with others the pressure to interact in a social way feels much less to me than it does in some other, less structured social situations. When birdwatching, there's no pressure to maintain conversation because if you do you're likely to see far fewer birds! Also, I find it easier to converse (when appropriate) because I know the people I am with are interested in and passionate about the same thing as me – birds, so it's much easier than having to try to think of what to say to a new person.

It was also recommended to me that as a birdwatcher, I

should set up a Twitter account. I promptly took on this advice and 'followed' a few large organisations and also some local birdwatchers whose names I'd heard mentioned. This proved to be a shrewd move, as Twitter is used very constructively by local birdwatchers and it helped me to find out more about local bird sightings and discuss local birdwatching sites. A survey respondent echoed this, writing that, 'A chance remark made me open a Twitter account to follow local birdwatchers. This in turn led to me meeting some of them and widening my circle of friends and acquaintances.'

At the opposite end of the birdwatching spectrum is twitching. I've been corrected by many people about the definition of twitching, so it's when you purposely go to see a bird that somebody else has found. Throughout 2015, I did just that, and spent a considerable amount of time touring the county at weekends with a birdwatcher who seemed to be motivated by achieving something. This is the hallmark of the achievement-oriented enthusiast – another category identified by the aforementioned study. They're involved in their activity primarily to meet some kind of standard or performance level. In this person's case they really enjoyed listing, which is literally keeping a listed record of all the birds you see.

Most birdwatchers tend to keep a list of every bird they've ever seen – usually called a life list. Or perhaps a record of every bird they've seen in a calendar year – a year list. Some keep lists for different locations, such as nature reserves, or perhaps their own garden. Some birdwatchers expand their listing a bit further and there are people that even keep 'TV lists' – literally a list of birds seen or heard in television programmes. A survey respondent showed how addictive listing can be, stating: 'I semi-obsessively keep lists of birds that I see and focus on trying to increase my patch list, patch year list, UK life list, UK year list and global life list.' That's an impressive list of lists.

Spending time with someone who enjoyed the listing approach gave me ample opportunity to compare and contrast our approaches to birdwatching. They were keen to add more species to their Norfolk year list, which invariably meant a considerable amount of (me) driving to new places. Adding species to my own list was fun and introduced me to lots of obscure birds, but I felt it detracted from the basic approach I'd started with. We also saw the same faces as we transferred to the next bird, or tick – as many birdwatchers refer to it (as they tick the bird off their proverbial list). This evoked a sense of the community within birdwatching, that collective interest, but it just never felt like the approach for me.

Record-keeping can be a positive activity, as I explore later, but if you already experience issues with obsessive behaviours or suffer with anxiety, it can be a negative one too. Listing can easily become the prime motivation for people to engage with birdwatching. I would argue, though, that they are not engaged with the act or art of birdwatching, more with the action of adding a bird to a list, collecting it, collating it and then moving on to the next. It all has an air of the innate hunter-gatherer instinct about it, don't you think?

Anyway, on 10 May 2015, something occurred that drastically changed how I felt about birdwatching and, more specifically, about twitching. I picked up my listing friend in the morning and from the moment they reached the car, I could see that they wore a palpable sense of excitement. 'Fancy a twitch, mate, citril finch?' they asked. This meant little to me, as in all honesty I didn't even know what a citril finch was. However, from my friend's eagerness in tone I knew it was a rhetorical question and that this bird would be our main agenda for the morning.

The bird, they explained as I drove, was the first of its kind on mainland Britain, with just one previous record from the Shetland Islands. I concurred that if it was that rare then we should probably go and see it, and we headed to Holkham in North Norfolk to walk out to Burnham Overy dunes, where the bird had last been seen. There was an obvious and significant increase in birdwatchers scurrying around the car park; their scopes worn on their backs – coupled with the green and tan tones of their field clothing – made them appear somewhat like a troop of infantrymen. We joined their purposeful march down the path next to the pine woods.

As we neared the last-reported site of the Iberian visitor, the amount of people grew drastically. Usually, large groups of people bother me little – if at all – but the frenetic edginess of this amassed crowd sent my anxiety into haywire. The next forty minutes or so was a maelstrom of moving limbs that were pointing and gesturing. I felt cramped and pressurised. The reality of the situation was that a small, hungry and lost bird was gradually being encircled by a gaggle of eager observers.

I was even unceremoniously lifted off my feet, by a brute of a birdwatcher who wanted me to finish my viewing so he could see for himself. He dumped me down to one side to clear a line of vision. This wasn't birdwatching – to me, anyway. The citril finch was, however, a lovely bird to look at. Not too dissimilar in shade to our resident greenfinches but with more yellow in the wing and a lead-grey back and nape.

There seemed to be a set of unwritten rules for this scenario, such as where it was appropriate to stand and what it was appropriate to say. It felt like an extreme manifestation of the affiliation-oriented birdwatcher, except there were hundreds of them! I felt stupidly edgy, and my heart rate and breathing had increased, but it wasn't due to any sort of positive adrenaline rush. I asked my friend if we could leave and they duly obliged, having also seen the bird.

We left the throng and moved to the tranquillity of a nearby bird hide, which happened to be empty. There we sat and talked about the experience, each recognising the other's perspective on twitching in large groups. I just couldn't fathom it and the pressure in my head had almost made me vomit. I vowed never to attend anything like that again. I knew that this was a very personal reaction, and I respect the positive aspects of activities like this. Travelling to new places, seeing the same faces and building up friendly rivalries has to be positive for the individuals concerned.

From that point onwards, I decided to enjoy birdwatching in the way I wanted to and not for the sake of numbers. I wanted to connect with nature on my own level. This is what constitutes the final category of wildlife enthusiast identified in the Canadian study, namely, appreciation-oriented. This type of enthusiast enjoys the peace, belonging and familiarity of their hobby or interest and the associated reduction in stress it brings them. This was me. I wanted my hobby to be a stress-reducing and calming activity. This would be my approach from now on.

The study also found that those birdwatchers who were identified as advanced were generally focused on the achievement side of birdwatching, whereas those who were identified as casual were more interested in the appreciative aspects of birdwatching. Perhaps this shows that the longer you're interested in birdwatching then the more likely it is that your motivations for doing it will change. This reflects my own experiences, although I've gone the opposite way and started off as a casual birdwatcher with a paradoxically achievement-oriented approach. As my attitude has changed, my approach seemed to organically develop into an appreciative one.

This is only my perspective though, and the act of listing is not entirely negative. As a way of keeping records to monitor the fate of birds on a local and national scale, it's a vital tool for scientists and conservationists. I've also found it useful for me in times of poor mental health, as it gives me another focus and outlet to channel my obsessiveness into. This helps to reduce the overall occurrences of anxiety and negativity in my personal and working lives, which has been pivotal in regaining focus in my life and career.

I received an interesting email from a birdwatcher who also had a negative view of twitching. They said they'd found it unhelpful as it released large amounts of adrenaline, which in turn led to addictive and obsessive tendencies and caused a heightened state of emotional behaviour – an unhealthy combination. The disappointment of missing out on a bird due to a failed twitch had a severe effect on their mood. This culminated in a bad twitch in the previous autumn, leading to a mild period of depression – and they almost gave up birdwatching entirely.

I suppose this could be an issue for any birdwatcher that twitches with the sole aim of increasing their list. The pressure to see birds for the sake of ticking them off, to me, could be dangerous for mental health, as outlined in the above example. I find that any situation where I place unnecessary pressure on myself to achieve something only serves to heighten my own anxiety, paranoia and low mood – especially if I don't meet the high expectations I usually set myself. This means that a full-on twitching or listing approach to birdwatching isn't an approach that I could ever have committed to from a health perspective either.

In order for people to be able to twitch rare birds, someone has to find them in the first place. In spring and autumn, rare vagrants can occur within movements of other migratory birds. I've never personally found a genuine rarity; a bird so rare that you have to submit descriptions and/or photographs to a committee, who decide if what you saw was what you said it was. These may be rarities on a county level or rare enough, nationally, to require validation by the British Birds Rarities Committee (BBRC) – the pinnacle of many birdwatchers' 'careers'.

Some birdwatchers dedicate their entire hobby to finding rare birds. They study weather conditions and patterns. They know where the best locations and habitats to check are. They often have years of experience and focus their efforts and attentions on singular, productive locations that repeatedly turn up rare birds. This has been described to me as the 'art' of rare bird finding and to quote one prolific rare bird finder I spoke to: 'Boy, is it an art!'

I wondered how and why these people became so focused on this approach, and this is how I came to speak to two people who identify, and are recognised, as rare bird finders. Firstly, I asked both of them what they felt their primary motivation was for finding rare birds – and neither felt that they could commit to one, singular reason why. In some ways, this reinforces my own views on the diverse appeal of birdwatching. One of them actually said that they needed to give me a 'multi-layered explanation' of their motivations, but both spoke of the experience and authenticity of searching for rarities. They also both shared the sense of achievement of finding a rare bird and the peer recognition this inevitably brings with it.

Most importantly, both talked about the skill and effort involved in their art. For the one who had spoken of the need for a multi-faceted answer this was a culmination of over thirty-five years of birdwatching field experience. They'd honed their understanding of the nuances of birds – from staring at dozens of bird books as a child to a stint as an assistant warden on a nature reserve. This innate desire to understand birds is our sixth sense. The birdwatcher's sense.

I also asked how it feels to find a rare bird, suspecting that seeking some kind of buzz was really why they did it. Neither mentioned adrenaline as I'd assumed they would, and both actually discussed the cognitive processes involved – of sorting out and adding up all the pieces of an avian identification jigsaw. This, one said, leads to a 'heady' moment, when the mind searches the subconscious for all the information gathered through years of observations, culminating in the final articulation of the species name.

To some, this element of uncertainty and suspense, albeit with a planned and desired outcome, may seem like the antithesis of the ethos of this book – yet the fundamentals are the same. Finding rare birds requires ultimate focus and dedication. It requires the observer to transcend into a state of being in tune with the land. Reading it and breathing it. In that sense, it's in harmony with mindfulness practice and my wider reflections on birdwatching. It may not be for everyone but it makes sense.

For the remainder of that year I began to refrain from

driving all over the county to add new birds to a list. After this, only a few of the trips my listing friend and I took together were to see specific species, and I started to realise that this approach to birdwatching was falling further and further back in terms of importance to me. I'm not saying that I don't enjoy looking at new species of birds – I just don't like the associated urgency of having a target. A summer spent engrossed in our beautiful native butterflies allowed me to separate myself even further from the listing approach, and as summer gradually faded into autumn I found myself falling back in love with my local area.

I started to birdwatch almost exclusively at local sites, meaning that I was no longer on the road, hunting down county rarities with my friend, and this meant I spent more time on my own. It wasn't entirely on purpose, it just seemed to happen that way – and I found tangible benefits in having time and space to reflect. I went birdwatching on a social basis a few times and the emphasis then was as much on social interaction as it was on the birds. That's not to say that I didn't enjoy the conversations, jokes and sharing of experiences – but through birdwatching alone I'd begun to forge a stronger, more tangible connection with the outdoors and with nature in general. I felt as though I was becoming a part of where I was. I actually wanted to enjoy it on my own.

This is what is known as a 'connection to nature' and seven of my survey respondents stated that they enjoyed 'connecting with nature', but what does that really mean? A friend of mine once said, 'We all need a bit of wilderness in us, mate,' and this sums it up fittingly. It's our own bit of innate wilderness and it's natural and intrinsic to our being. The dictionary definition of connecting includes feeling an affinity with something, and it's this affinity and closeness to nature that brings us such pleasure. Within the survey sat a beautiful quote about connecting with nature: 'The fact is that modern life in cities with nothing but stark grey isn't how the human animal was designed to live, and though we obsess over money and things, actually what matters is remembering that nature isn't a place you should visit, it's your origin. It is you.'

A social media connection, again, provided me with a platform to ask others what *they* thought connecting to nature really meant. The consensus was that there are many ways to approach this statement, from the ecological to the artistic. A notion repeated several times was that it's feeling a 'part' of nature, with one respondent stating specifically that it was about 'feeling an integral part of nature'. Another stated that, 'Connecting with nature is awakeness; the mind is calm, at peace, then you are living in the moment, aware of everything.'

This fits with the ideologies of mindfulness. Jon Kabat-Zinn, whose work most modern, mindful stress-reduction therapies are based around, defines mindfulness as 'paying attention, on purpose, in the present moment, and non-judgementally'.[4] When applied to birdwatching practice there are evident correlations. You pay attention in a particular and focused manner, not just on birds, but also on the wider environment. It's very much a purposeful pastime, as it can be accessed almost everywhere. It grounds us in the present moment – here and now, and unless you have heavily entrenched motivations, as discussed earlier, it's a wholly non-judgemental hobby.

Another approach to birdwatching that I discovered can be extremely mindful is sea watching. Sea watching involves exactly what its name implies – watching the sea. Depending on which coastline you're on, strong winds can blow different and exciting birds past you. On the Norfolk coast it's a brisk northerly that birdwatchers eagerly await, pushing birds down and around the curve of the county. The majority of sea watching is performed through a birdwatching scope, essentially a portable telescope, offering the user higher magnification and a wider objective lens. A scope offers the same cocooning of the peripheral vision as binoculars do, although it seems even more focused and intense.

The tumultuous sound of waves crashing on to shingle coupled with the seemingly endless view of the churning water creates a very insular feeling. You almost become at one with the situation and this feeling of connection is enhanced even further when you're wrapped up warm against the cold; although you can still feel the icy blast of the wind, lashing against your cheeks as they're licked by the occasional splash of salt spray.

My first proper sea watch stays with me. I spent the morning at Weybourne in the esteemed company of a close friend, scanning the North Sea in relatively choppy conditions. The waves gave us wonderful views of a plethora of species. We were treated to incredibly close passes by of nature's pirates – great and Arctic skuas. We also saw the powerful, wave-shearing flight of Manx and sooty shearwaters. It was blissful and momentous.

I fell in love with the sea that day and realised what an exhilarating experience I'd been missing out on. The way I became so attuned to the surroundings was comprehensive and, although complex, still relaxing. It was a true multi-sensory experience, of salt-speckled lips, foamy white wave crests and the sound of the sea's power as it pounded the beach.

I wish to share with you a single experience that unites all the strands of connection. It was a late-July evening, warm but not hot, and a post-work foray to Cley Marshes NWT had been arranged, to meet a friend. They had spoken of an evening influx of wading birds and gulls coming in to roost on islets in the reserve's lagoons – something for us to savour and share. There we were, sitting in a hide overlooking Pat's Pool. It was a gorgeous evening – calm and serene – with a stunning sunset falling behind us, casting pinkish reflections on to the still silvery waters.

We conversed, we laughed and we observed. Together. There were so many birds pottering about on the two scrapes. Eleven green sandpipers fed in front of us, skittish and probing. Earlier we'd counted three curlew sandpipers, still wearing the remnants of their brick-red breeding plumage. Further away wasn't just one, but four roosting yellow-legged gulls, their heads tucked under their wings, motionless.

As dusk loomed ever closer, there were pleasant surprises to be shared too. Three Arctic terns flew high over us before eight spoonbills dropped on to an adjacent pool to preen. An ethereal barn owl closed the ceremony of birds with a nearby fly-past, ghosting over the reeds in the foreground.

This is just a snapshot of the scarcer birds that we saw and shared that night, without even mentioning the commoner species. What a beautiful way to spend an evening: connecting with a friend, laughing, joking and sharing an experience; connecting with a plethora of bird species, observing, enjoying and recording; connecting with a sensational environment, living, breathing and feeling. Connecting in so many ways and on so many levels – priceless, memorable and powerful.

A few practical tips about connecting through birdwatching

Consider using social media to engage with other birdwatchers and to share your sightings. Twitter seems to be the most popular platform for this.

Investigate local bird groups or clubs, as they can widen your local birdwatching network with others who share your interest.

Try to talk to people that you see when out birdwatching – they may end up becoming a birdwatching acquaintance. Wear your binoculars with pride!

Experience birdwatching with others when you can, as more eyes and ears can potentially mean more birds.

Consider finding yourself a local birdwatching patch. The consistency and security that visiting a regular patch provides can also help you to connect with yourself and with nature. There's more on this later.

VI.

An egret, a kingfisher and remembering to feed the birds

'The best way to find yourself is to lose yourself in the service of others' – Mahatma Gandhi

ike all hobbies, the primary outcome of birdwatching is to gain something for the hobbyist. This could be the adding of a tick to a list, the enjoyment of visiting a new place or, as in my own case, for relaxation. This varies according to the individual and their motivations, and by differing levels of engagement, commitment and dedication; but it doesn't have to be all about gaining something. There are indeed many accessible ways for anyone to take their interest full-circle if they wish to.

Giving, helping, supporting, random acts of kindness – whatever you choose to call it, it's good for your health and wellbeing. This was documented in 'Doing good?', a report by the Mental Health Foundation exploring the benefits of helping others. It found that helping others can improve morale, self-esteem, happiness and wellbeing, and reduces depressive symptoms. It also helps people to develop positive self-identity as a 'good' person.[1]

I asked through social media what people felt they'd given back to birdwatching, and their general reply was that they 'fed the birds'. Bird feeding is, in my opinion, the most accessible way to not only assist birds with their survival, but also to enhance the opportunity to engage with them. You don't even need access to a large outside space to start attracting birds close to home, due to the advent of things like window-mounted feeders and readily available ground-feeding seed mixes.

When we first bought our house, I was keen to get my bird feeders set up as soon as possible, as I'd been spoiled by the garden at our previous residence, in suburban Norwich. The avian highlight was when I heard the unmistakable '*zi-zit*' call of a grey wagtail from upstairs, with the windows open. I couldn't see the pond so ran downstairs at full pelt and out of the back door. There on the ornamental waterfall for a fleeting moment, all luscious lemon tones and bobbing tail, sat a gorgeous grey wagtail, before flying off, never to visit the garden again.

Within minutes of my feeders being positioned at the new house, three house sparrows and a blue tit tentatively edged down the willow tree that hung over the fence. What was this new food source that had just appeared? They flicked hesitantly across to investigate, visiting one by one and taking a seed as they went. This was to be the blossoming of a growing relationship between me and my garden visitors. Me, providing them with food – and them, providing me with comfort and consistency.

There are many things that you can do to attract more birds to an outdoor space and I would start by spending some time getting to know your bird community. As well as being one of the best ways to develop your basic birdwatching knowledge, it can also be very insightful. Through grasping what types of birds are visiting, you can ensure that you provide them the best food. For example, if your most abundant bird family are finches, then seed mixes are the best food to provide. I learned that although most of my visiting birds were partial to seed mix, they also loved to tuck into a suet product or three.

The sparrows and tits had been regularly visiting my 'trial' suet balls and had polished them off in less than a week, so I decided to stock them up. I put out three suet fat balls in a mesh feeder and also bought a suet-block cage to try out too. The following morning, I was awoken at seven by a witch-like din of screeching and cackling from the back garden. What on earth was it? I ran down the stairs to find out, clutching at my dressing gown as I whipped it around my shoulders hastily.

I reached the French doors and could immediately see the culprits. Eleven shimmering starlings were writhing across my feeders, jostling and snapping at each other as they decimated the suet block and balls. I watched on, amazed, as they fought over every crumb that dropped to the floor. It was brilliant that they were using and accessing the food I'd provided for them, but at the same time I became very aware of the cacophony they were making at an early hour. I slid open the door and as I did so, the starlings all took flight at the same time in a flurry of wings, speckles and iridescence. This gave me an opportunity to swiftly remove the offending suet items and stow them away indoors. OK, so suet products would have to be used sparingly from now on.

I once had a conversation with another birdwatcher about their own garden bird feeding habits, and they regaled me with tales of marsh tits and even a great spotted woodpecker visiting them. Enviously, I asked what their secret was and they said, 'Peanuts and sunflower hearts.' What did I do? I went and bought some – filling one feeder up with peanuts and one with sunflower hearts, along with my usual seed mix. The peanuts didn't prove as popular as I'd hoped; they stagnated in their feeder for a few weeks, mouldy and darkened and I eventually removed them.

The sunflower hearts, though, would be full when I left for work in the morning and empty when I returned. It took several refills and a weekend stakeout before I could identify the culprit(s). I sat on a dining-room chair, cup of tea in hand, and watched the feeding station from my front row seat by the door. A handful of house sparrows, two blue tits, a lone great tit and finally a coal tit, all descended upon the hearts at once. Everyone seemed to want some.

The coal tit, it could've been Colin, whipped in and deftly extracted a heart, before popping on to the fence and stashing it between panels. I watched him repeat this action three times before zipping away over my neighbour's garden. Observing this moment was fascinating and it demonstrated an avian nuance that one doesn't often get to see. What a resourceful way of preserving food this was – we often forget just how intelligent and adaptable birds can be.

Occasionally my dedication to feeding our garden bird community seemed to pay off. Our bathroom skylight gives an eye-level view of the top of an overhanging willow, and one morning I was brushing my teeth when, out of the corner of my eye, I spied a bird in its upper branches. It was a portly blush-peach bird with a charcoal cap, which I knew was a female bullfinch. It was a splendid start to my day and set me up with a positive mindset. I'm happy to see a bullfinch anywhere – both males and females are stunning birds – yet to see one in my own garden felt even more of a treat; like just rewards for giving something back.

Feeding birds in your garden was formally recognised as an activity that promotes positive wellbeing in 2016. Daniel Cox and Kevin J. Gaston of the University of Exeter published a research paper on this very topic and found that their participants' overall wellbeing improved when they noticed the birds in their garden.[2] They also discussed their participants' perceptions of feeling connected with nature through doing so. Furthermore, they considered whether maintaining and watching bird feeders over time could help to reduce stress. The research also pointed towards 'increased self-reported feelings of relaxation'.

I'm incredibly thankful to my local bird group for offering me a very different opportunity to give something back, when they rallied for volunteers to help at a local wildlife event, and as a teacher, I jumped at the opportunity to enthuse others about birds. This entailed a couple of hours manning a display stand and facilitating a children's 'guess the bird' quiz, followed by a stint being a 'guide in a hide'. Both opportunities allowed me to utilise my professional skills and combine them with my personal interest.

It was a privilege to witness children's eyes light up whilst looking at an owl from a local sanctuary, or when they correctly guessed the name of a lesser-known garden bird in our quiz. At an event like this, many people will walk past you and pay minimal attention, but if one in every ten stops and talks to you, connections can be made. Sharing an interest does not mean that you must be engaged on the same level – sometimes it's those little sparks that linger the longest.

It can be hugely fulfilling to encourage young people to take an interest in nature and, in my opinion, it's the most rewarding way to give something back to the wider environment. Remember that through providing enthusiasm and inspiration, the foundations for future birdwatchers and nature enthusiasts are laid. I often wonder whether more serious birdwatchers, like those who are competitively listing, ever pause their hectic schedules of twitching to show a young person what all those clad in pseudo army fatigues are pointing their big lenses at?

I love to have a bird hide to myself, as I'm sure most birdwatchers do. But, if a family walks in behind me and an excited child clambers up on to the bench, the last thing

I would do is tut and make them feel uncomfortable. I've witnessed this a lot and I don't think anyone should have to apologise for a child's enthusiasm and inquisitiveness. I always go out of my way to converse with them, tell them what I've seen and offer them the use of my optical equipment and my understanding.

This exact scenario played out when I was on my stint as a guide in a hide. I was at Pensthorpe Natural Park, near Fakenham: a managed wildlife park with many captive birds (predominantly wildfowl) and a lovely scrape at the far end of it. A scrape is just as it sounds; the land is literally scraped away and then backfilled with water, in the hope of attracting birds to it. Scrapes provide enticing stop-off points for migrating wading birds and wildfowl. I imagine they appear as glittering oases of food and shelter when approached from above. They often have islands or spits within that can provide places for refuge, rest and even for breeding.

The hide was one of two, appearing at a distance like little boxes wrapped in parcel paper. I made myself comfortable on the bench and set my scope up to survey the scrape with. Even though it was crammed full of birds, it was still incredibly tranquil. Time to have a look through the… A bang. The door had swung open and collided with the hide wall behind me. Two boys bowled in, maybe eight years old, possibly brothers and closely followed by two adults who I assumed were their parents. 'We're so sorry,' they said to me – I guess they thought I would be irked by the disturbance.

'Please don't be sorry,' I replied. 'Come in and see what you can spot!'

I lowered my scope and focused on a little egret that was strutting along the reed fringe in front of us. 'Have a look at this,' I said.

One of the boys came over and looked into the eyepiece. 'Wow, that's cool!'

The other followed and looked. 'It's a white heron!'

I commended him for his reasoned guess and turned around, gesturing both to look at the large wall chart behind me that depicted the main species of bird seen from the hide. I asked them which one they thought it was. They both looked and mulled it over, then simultaneously pointed at an image of a little egret. I gave them much praise before they lost interest, as children invariably do, and made to leave.

'Thanks for that,' said the father.

'My pleasure,' was my honest reply.

It was invigorating to see the spark of excitement that came from those two boys, looking at something closely and then determining its identity from a range of options. It was learning in action and it reaffirmed just why I love birdwatching. A correspondent on social media wrote that a birdwatcher should 'spread their passion far and wide' and on that day, that's exactly what I was able to do.

One place that I never expected to be able to spread my passion was at work. I've written about work previously – teaching children who've been excluded from mainstream education. It may come as a surprise that some of my most rewarding birdwatching experiences have been at work or whilst I've been on off-site visits with students. Two of these experiences linger strongly in my mind.

The first took place in a car full of obnoxious and rowdy fifteen-year-old boys. A car that was being driven by me, their teacher and chauffeur. I was counting down the miles until we reached our destination, an activity centre in mid-Norfolk, where we would be braving high-ropes and racing Segways. It was a twenty-five-minute drive and halfway through the journey I'd fallen into one of those driving trances, washed over by the relentless chatter around me. Suddenly, out of nowhere, a large raptor took flight from the field to our right.

Howls of incredulity filled the car as a red kite drifted across the road and over us. 'That's a red kite,' I informed them, which was followed by a free-flowing discussion about its size, shape and majesty. They'd paid specific attention to its forked tail and I was secretly impressed that they'd noticed this detail. Throughout the remainder of that academic year, one of the students would often ask me if I remembered 'that kite' and I knew it had stayed with him as it had with me. It was an electric moment, when a noble and graceful bird had imprinted itself in the memories of a group of young people.

The second experience is one that I often speak about and I've even given it a name – the kingfisher analogy. This was the experience that really started to shape my ideas about using birdwatching as a therapeutic tool with other people, and not just me. It started with a student who wasn't having a great day, so I offered to remove him from the situation for a personal tutorial. It was a lovely day, so I asked if he wanted to go for a walk and conduct his tutorial either outdoors or in a café, to which he agreed. Our destination was nearby Whitlingham Country Park, a reclaimed gravel pit that's now a country park, activity centre and wildlife haven.

I parked the car, paid for the privilege, and retrieved two pairs of binoculars out of my car boot, as I always carried a spare pair in case of moments like this. It was May, that awkward season where the weather can't seem to decide if it wants to be cold or mild. Rainfall on the day before meant that the ground squelched underfoot and, precious about his branded trainers, he scolded and muttered as he danced round muddy puddles. A few minutes into our walk, whilst we strolled leisurely through a thin strip of young woodland, he was introduced to the melodious warble of a blackcap. The skulking silver songster sat low and hidden, so we waited for it to appear. My student seemed patient, slightly unlike him, and I noticed that he seemed calmer whilst we watched, waited and chatted.

Our walk continued towards Little Broad, the aptly named smaller of the park's two waterbodies. Stopping at its edge, we spent some time observing the range of wildfowl that were lounging on the water. I started to count them out loud. 'The silver ones, they're gadwall,' I told him, and he began to count along with me. I explained my childhood connection with the great crested grebe, as we watched one strafe and dive. He seemed to recognise the emotional links I described. For a short while, we spoke no words and just observed through our binoculars, blocking out the outside world and absorbing the pacifying qualities of nature.

The silence was shattered by his animated shouting: 'Oh my god! What's that?' I followed his gaze and glimpsed a kingfisher flying over the lake in front of us, no more than six inches above the surface. This shimmering blue-and-orange bird, skimming across the water, was a reasonably common sight for me. However, for a teenager growing up in one of the most deprived areas of Norfolk this was pure magic, and I could see that magic etched across his face and burning in his eyes.

He was energised by the experience, excitedly asking me about kingfishers and extracting what I knew. 'How long have we been out for?' he asked.

'About twenty minutes,' I replied.

'Wow, I feel like we've been out here for at least an hour!' he mused.

At the time, I didn't think much of what he'd said, but a year on as I sit writing this on Cromer beach, bathed in glorious sunshine with fulmars gliding and soaring above my head, I recognise its significance.

The kingfisher analogy may end up being a once-in-a-lifetime experience for him. How powerful is that? How therapeutic had nature been that day, in slowing down his chaotic mind to enable him to perhaps feel at ease for a moment? I have given talks on Bird Therapy, and this analogy is a core element of what I say, with the underpinning notion that if birdwatching and nature can have such a profound impact on that one young person, then can that magic be harnessed to help others too?

There are also some less person-centred ways to give something back. Approaches that are focused more on conservation, or on having an input to a wider network of contributors. For any birdwatcher or nature enthusiast who regularly observes the same area, the keeping of notes and records can be a wonderful thing. It allows you to build up a picture of the birdlife and if you continue to observe that site over a period of years, it then enables you to monitor ongoing trends and patterns.

Each year in my home county of Norfolk, wildlife enthusiasts are treated to the annual 'Norfolk Bird and Mammal Report', courtesy of the Norfolk and Norwich Naturalists' Society (NNNS). First published in 1953, these reports are a treasure trove of information, cataloguing nature sightings by date and volume and providing a comprehensive anthology of Norfolk's birds. When I first started birdwatching a friend loaned me the previous year's report. It was fascinating and I really had no idea about the breadth of avifauna that visited the county.

More importantly though, it showed me that every scrap of data that local enthusiasts collected serves a wider purpose in mapping the avian life of Norfolk, past and present. I wanted to be involved, to feel a connection and be part of something. So, at the end of my first full year as a dedicated birdwatcher, I took great delight in compiling and submitting my records, spanning many visits to the coast, along with my stoic local observations. Not only was it exciting to reflect on the previous year's experiences but it was also incredibly cathartic to go through this process. It was a diary of experience, journaling towards wellness.

The methodical organising and compiling of my records created a tangible outcome to my birdwatching forays. It unlocked my birdwatching memory vault and gave me a purpose that made me feel good. I could lose myself for hours, compiling information and forgetting everything else, as I relived a high flock count or a scarce local visitor. It served as a distraction, an obsession, that reduced impact in other areas.

When I posed my earlier question about giving something back to birdwatching, a correspondent remarked that bird feeding had been mentioned by many – but what about citizen science? If you aren't aware of the term, the *National Geographic* encyclopaedia defines it as 'the practice of public participation and collaboration in scientific research to increase scientific knowledge'.[3] Submitting bird records for the purposes of annual collation certainly fits with this definition and, although not always scientific, the patterns and trends that these records produce are a dataset of immense value.

If you want to use your interest in birds to contribute to citizen science, there are many initiatives available to you. The main bird and nature organisations all have their own schemes on offer, like the RSPB's Big Garden Birdwatch, an annual event that's so much more than just an hour in the garden, counting birds (see my own epiphanic encounter with that dunnock). The British Trust for Ornithology (BTO) also run a weekly survey called the Garden BirdWatch scheme, where participants record the highest frequency of a species in their garden at roughly the same time each week.

These home-based citizen science projects feed into wider networks. Networks of positive interactions. Networks that share individual snapshots of avian garden life. Networks that channel them into an overview of how our garden birds are faring nationwide. They also provide an accessible way for people to connect with nature at home, creating an opportunity to become more attuned to local wildlife.

The BTO also conduct a range of other surveys covering various areas such as breeding birds, wetlands and estuaries. These require the surveyor to hold a certain level of bird identification skill and are a vital form of citizen science, leading to detailed scientific research and reports. I decided that I wanted to get involved and looked in to the range of local schemes on offer. The first opportunity that arose was to take on a stretch of the Norfolk coastline for a NEWS, or Non-Estuarine Waterbird Survey. I was allocated a sector that covered Horsey in East Norfolk.

With the February survey window approaching, I

foolishly forgot that my survey date would fall at the height of seal season in Norfolk. Horsey, along with Blakeney Point, North Norfolk, is home to a huge colony of breeding grey seals. These are a major tourist attraction that draws in many visitors, as the adults raise their pups on the beach. Engrossed in the new school term I almost forgot about the seals, until the day of the survey was upon me and I went out to conduct it.

Stepping out on to the strandline filled me with vigour. The placid sea was lapping against the shore, before receding back through smooth pebbles, making a sound like a rain-stick being tipped. The late-winter sun sat low in the sky, bathing all in a warm glow, and the beach lay starkly beautiful in front of me. If the view was impressive then the sight of the seals was mesmerising. As far as the eye could see lay seals of all shapes and sizes, lolling around on the beach in unbelievable numbers.

Aside from all this talk about seals (in my sector alone, I stopped counting at five hundred!), there were birds there too. I spent some time watching a handful of sanderlings running back and forth along the shoreline. A literal handful; a tiny sanderling would fit snugly into the palm of your hand. These dainty wading birds are a joy to behold in both their summer and winter plumages. These were in their winter plumage: icy-white below, rusty-grey above and with a short black bill. As they scurried between the lazy seals, they looked so small and delicate. The seals weren't bothered by them at all.

The morning survey at Horsey whetted my appetite for citizen science. Even though there were plenty of people there for the seals, I still felt remarkably alone. Not alone in a negative sense, but alone in the sense of feeling at one with my environment. I craved to experience this feeling again, so I researched if there were any other local opportunities I could partake in. This led me back to the BTO and to their Wetland Bird Survey (WeBS).

WeBS is a monthly count of the wetland birds that are present on a specified waterbody. The counts are coordinated on the same day nationwide and this helps to map trends, not just locally, but on a national scale too. I knew a few people who conducted these at their own local patches, so I looked on the map of registered sites and discovered that the main lake at my patch wasn't one and had never been. A few emails later and my beloved patch was also a registered WeBS site, and, due to my stringent record-keeping and slightly obsessive visiting patterns, I was able to backdate the counts to the start of the year, laying solid foundations to build upon.

There was a tangible feeling of purpose and responsibility that came from doing these surveys and these feelings are good for your wellbeing. A study into the idea of purpose, by Larissa Rainey of Pennsylvania University, deduced that there are five 'ingredients' to purpose. Two are particularly relevant to birdwatching: that it provides direction and creates goals for the future and that it provides a benefit and/or connection to someone or something other than the self.[4]

We know that birdwatching can provide direction and goals for many people, especially when twitching and listing. I've also known people who've specialised in learning about one bird family, such as woodpeckers. Me, I longed to be part of something and to feel a sense of connection and community; and my monthly count did just that. I was part of a network, a web of other people who, on the same day, were also scanning flocks of wildfowl on a local lake, dreaming of a rare grebe paddling out of the reed fringes. It made me feel good that I was part of an initiative. A citizen scientist.

As well as having a count to look forward to every month, it also strengthened the bond I have with the park. The more time I found myself spending there, the more positive I felt in general. These feelings of consistency and purpose were having a positive impact on my wellbeing, helping to curb the inflated sense of responsibility that I often tarnish my everyday life with. This also led to an uplift in my writing and a clarity of thought and process – enhancing my goal to share my message about the therapeutic benefits of birdwatching with as many people as possible.

Birdwatching also provides numerous opportunities for altruistic actions. Whether that's inspiring the next generation or sharing sightings, it connects you to 'someone or something other than the self', as Rainey describes it, even when that connection is with birds, or their environment. What was essentially just an hour spent counting some ducks became part of my Bird Therapy.

A final note on Rainey's study: she wrote that, 'Many participants noted the importance of curiosity, exploration, and self-acceptance in finding their purpose.' These three affective areas are important elements of birdwatching too. It's not a stereotypically trendy hobby and one has to be accepting of that, but for the best part its culture is accepting, thus promoting self-acceptance. To watch birds and learn about them, we are explorers, and how can you not associate birdwatching with curiosity? We watch birds to find out more about their lives – because we're curious about them in the first place.

My survey reaffirmed the positivity of engaging with bird surveys. From a hundred random respondents, sixteen specifically mentioned bird surveying as a fundamental part of their overall birdwatching experience. One respondent stood out, saying that they took part in over twenty different survey and citizen science initiatives. My overall research indicates that those who classify themselves as serious birdwatchers often partake in surveying, or volunteer at their local reserve. This can only strengthen connections with nature through spending more time at the places you love.

I finish with an experience that doesn't begin as a wholly bird-orientated one, but certainly highlights the immense value in giving and sharing. It was high summer at my patch and the eutrophic water of both lakes had burst into life. A luscious layer of greenery was encouraging a plethora of damselflies and dragonflies to skim over the lake surface. If I kneeled at the water's edge, I was able to watch them with great interest and amusement and it was, perhaps, the first time I'd properly stopped and taken notice of them.

It was a damselfly. Small, black and iridescent blue was its body and it had large and wide-set red eyes. I was sure it was a small red-eyed damselfly, a relatively scarce species that a few people had been discussing on social media lately. I shared a picture and swiftly received confirmation from others that it was what I thought it was. Soon after, I received a private message from someone asking if I would be willing to show him. Of course, I obliged this request and we met one warm afternoon to investigate.

I know little about Odonata (the term for dragonflies and damselflies) and as we looked at the large numbers congregating near a miniature sluice gate, he amazed me with his ability to identify them so quickly, telling me little facts about them as he did. We moved on, stopping to look at some butterflies on a momentous buddleia bush I'd found the previous week. We walked, talked and shared our interest and it was brilliant. As we ambled along the lakeside path, we were treated to two hobbies hawking over the main lake. They were an absolute delight and he revelled in taking photos of them as they strafed the lake like fighter jets. These zebra-striped falcons with their blood-red undertail coverts were just beautiful. There's no other word for them. I felt so lucky.

I'd given him access to my own pocket of wildlife and he'd given me his wisdom and company in return. He also shared a wonderful photo of a hobby with me later.

The entire visit was a bilateral and unifying occasion, encapsulating the reciprocity of birdwatching and nature in general. Both are gifts and both keep on giving. My final gift here is to leave you, as always, with some practical tips about giving something back through birdwatching.

A few practical tips about giving something back through birdwatching

The best way to give something back to birdwatching is to provide food and water for your bird community. The RSPB, Wildlife Trusts and the BTO all provide guidance about how to get the most out of garden bird feeding.

Share your wisdom – it can be inspirational, especially when younger generations are involved. Also, allow people to look through your scope or binoculars at a distant bird – it's like opening a new world for them.

Keep and submit your bird records as they can help to map local and national data trends, as well as potentially encouraging others to monitor and visit different areas.

Engage in citizen science, as it's vitally important for monitoring birds. The RSPB and BTO facilitate national garden birdwatching initiatives, which are a superb starting point. The BTO also deliver a range of nationwide surveys via volunteers and these can be a wonderful way of dedicating yourself to a specific location and learning more about it.

VII.

A local patch, two diving ducks and a mountain blackbird

'Place is security, space is freedom' – Yi-Fu Tuan

I t's widely regarded that the idea of watching a local patch was first written about in the seminal book *The Natural History of Selborne* by naturalist and pastor Gilbert White.[1] First published in 1789, it's a treasured tome considered by many to be one of the finest pieces of nature writing ever written. With its rambling layout, it's not always an easy book to read, but if you persevere with his wonderful and often naive descriptions and relish in his stoic observations, then the pages will reveal White's world to you. Selborne – his parish and his patch.

In *A Bird in the Bush*, Stephen Moss's brilliant book about the social history of birdwatching, White's influential work is noted as being quite different from anything that came before it. Perhaps more pertinently, Moss states that *Selborne* has stood the test of time because, even now, we can identify with White's desire to spend time with the natural world and gain spiritual refreshment from doing so.[2]

What exactly is a patch? It would be narrow-minded to define the term from just my own thoughts, so I invited people, through social media, to share their own definitions. The consensus was that a patch is an area or location, of any size, that a birdwatcher (or naturalist) visits and observes on a regular basis. Regularity is important and Moss touches upon this when he writes that visiting a local patch in this way allows you to tune into the daily, monthly and seasonal rhythms of life. A patch can become a microcosm of these motions and changes – as we shall see.

The end of 2015 and a new birdwatching year was almost upon us. After much cajoling from a friend, I'd signed up for an initiative called the Patchwork Challenge. We'd had many conversations about it at my friend's own patch, Sparham Pools, which although it was a fantastic site, we were both loath to share. This was because the principle of the Patchwork Challenge is competition. One where points are scored for all the species of bird seen within a defined area, with the scores then displayed in regional league tables. The defined area, your patch, had to cover no more than three square kilometres, but could be any shape; and yes, there were some obtusely shaped patches.

I spoke about this with some other birdwatchers, who shared mixed views. Some believed it was childish folly to turn birdwatching into a game, and others, with more entrenched motivations for birdwatching, thought it unwise to focus so pointedly on one area. 'You should be up the coast finding rare birds,' was the usual rebuttal. Yet this was what *they* wanted to do – it was *their* approach to *their* hobby. I was still determined to forge my own path.

Yes, there are increased odds of finding rarer birds at coastal migration sites and, yes, rare bird finders are held in reverence – with some achieving almost mythical status. Some people thrive off this: the adrenaline, the back-slapping and the high-fives. It requires absolute dedication and copious amounts of time though. Attributes that don't always fit in with life commitments. Doesn't this also add a somewhat unnecessary pressure to what is, fundamentally, a passive pastime?

Besides, bird migration hotspots can be overrun at weekends, and not just by birdwatchers searching for that elusive rare wanderer. These places are often areas of outstanding natural beauty and people visit them for touristic and aesthetic reasons too. This can make them the antithesis of a relaxing place and a few visits to somewhere like the Norfolk coast, in peak season, can be off-putting for many.

My patch had to be local, as not only was my affinity with the area growing, but also if a patch was closer to home then it would encourage me to visit regularly. If this was the first criterion for deciding on a patch, then the second was to find somewhere under-watched so I could take some ownership. It's not easy to do this with a well-watched site like a wildlife reserve as they exist to protect, share and promote the wildlife within them. Therefore, they are there for everyone to enjoy and are often oversubscribed.

This shared ownership is a powerful thing, but as with any relationship, the more people that are involved, the more difficult it becomes – too many cooks, as they say.

My search began with the unfurling of an Ordnance Survey map. The crackle of pleated sheets and the scent of knowledge flooded over me. As did the mesmerising sight of a vast miniature world settling on the living-room carpet, with its graceful grid squares of order and logic. Maps have been a lifelong fascination of mine and there's an intrinsic magic about the curves and contours of your local area condensed into a two-dimensional illustration.

I thought of our nationally heralded wildlife reserves, which all feature an abundance of habitats interwoven into webs of sustenance. My patch needed habitats and preferably as many as possible, for surely this would bring me the most variety of bird species? Whilst scanning the map, a nearby lake leaped out at me – just a blue-washed, stomach-shaped blot on the map paper. It seemed to be part of a hall park, with its north-east edge annexed by a vast area of woodland. It sat just spitting distance from my familiar heathlands and possible amalgamations occurred in my mind. A patch was starting to form.

The hall park turned out to be a private chalet park and at this point it would've been easy to give up and return to the map. Something had clicked inside me though and an attachment had begun to form, just from mentally exploring the site. I was certain that this was to be my patch. My thoughts became imagery – the sun shimmering on the still, silver waters of the lake and slicing through the forest rides in high summer. Would access be granted? A telephone call – a friendly discussion – would it be OK if I came in and had a look to see what birdlife was around the park? Of course – I could go anywhere – how lucky and how kind.

The park manager and I became acquainted shortly after that conversation took place. It was late in the year, yet it seemed only natural to carry out a few reconnaissance forays before the challenge started. In mid-December, my first ever visit took place and in terms of avian diversity it was uneventful. More importantly though, a connection was made with the manager who had granted me access in the first place. He shared a walking route with me that took in the best areas of the park and he was excited to find out about the extent of the birdlife there, as it hadn't been studied before – at least in anything other than a recreational capacity.

This initial visit didn't really shine a light on the resident birds though, with only a sparse selection of wildfowl and common birds around the park. Looking back, I realise that was to be expected at that time of the year, with my intention always being to get to know the geography of the location, not to scrutinise it. In keeping with this notion, the second visit, a week later, was much more productive as familiarity crept in.

Notes from that day fill a much larger writing space, counts appear more methodical and the number of species seen was much greater. The notes remained meagre though and perhaps showed that an attachment hadn't begun to forge itself at that point. I was still visiting Sparham Pools and had even referred to it as 'Sparham patch' in my notebook, but this was soon to change.

The new year rolled in and on its second day came my inaugural patch ramble. It was a crisp morning, with every exhalation billowing about like pipe smoke. The shrubbery on the approach to the lake glistened with diamanté frosting and the icy avenue was still and quiet – a stark paradox to the clamour of Christmas and New Year. It was a blank canvas and my records from that day make for interesting reading. A wider range of birds were observed, and accurate counts reflect a thorough and more focused walk. A little egret was the undoubted highlight, holding an almost mythical status there now.

Another January surprise came the following weekend, in the form of a fine water bird, a goosander. It was the first bird I saw that morning, as it darted purposefully across the ornamental lake. This drake, with his bottle-green head and clean-white body, was a joy to behold. A hunched and vaguely reptilian bird armed with a saw-like bill, the origin of their collective family name 'sawbills'. Goosanders can turn up on any inland body of water during winter, but turning up there, so soon after getting to know the place – it carried a certain significance.

The following month brought fresh surprises. My records note several new birds for the park including the first of many kingfisher sightings – a bird with an iconic resonance in this story. Similarly the skylark, also a new bird that month, heard serenading over the adjacent fields. Every visit yielded impressive numbers of gadwall – fifties and sixties. These ducks are always worth a second look, as when viewed in overcast light they appear drab, but when you catch a drake in direct sunlight you find yourself being dazzled as their grey feathers reflect metallic silver.

A few months passed and I found myself treading a familiar circuit around the lake and the woods. As spring blossomed, I found the magnetism of the coast too hard to resist, and off I went again, neglecting my patch in search of new birds to tick off on my tentative flirtation with a year list. My efforts were being channelled into seeing as many birds as I feasibly could, and I still sought acceptance and interaction, which, sadly, led to a general lack of appreciation for my local area. It took the citril finch incident, coupled with the breaking of several negative thought processes, for things to actually change.

It was almost a whole year before I reconnected. I spent the first winter period visiting various sites up and down the Wensum Valley but not the patch. I'd neglected it and would never know what may have dropped in there throughout the year. It was the week before Christmas and a strange compulsion was growing inside me, a feeling that the park needed me and I needed it too. I popped in for a fleeting visit and was buoyed by the spectacle of a roving tit flock – skittish, yet directed in their movements – their high frequency contact calls enveloping me. This was a brief visit though, an after-work foray, and a few days later, the patch and I were reacquainted properly.

It was Christmas Eve and I had another urge, but this time it was to go to the lake. The sky loomed dreary and overcast and the wintry clouds hung heavy, as did the dew on the ferns in the Great Wood. On the lake surface writhed an ivory mass, constantly altering its shape and throwing out the sharpness of wings and bills. One – two – a slow and methodical count. There were 167 black-headed gulls loafing there, decimating my previous highest count. Almost a year to the day it was chosen as my patch, it felt like the land was giving me a signal, and the patch flame was reignited like an advent candle.

As the new year arrived, it was set up to be a pivotal one for me, my hobby and the development of my patch. After the previous year's maelstrom of emotions over my motivations, my entire approach to birdwatching was shifting. A determination grew, to treat the patch with the respect it deserved, to strengthen both our relationship and my connection with nature. I yearned to watch the land transform with every season, as Gilbert White had done with his beloved Selborne. I knew it meant increased dedication and visits but surely it would be more rewarding? I was ready to commit to the land I loved.

The bitter bite of February, cold and sharp. I was working from home, planning lessons and generally feeling trapped by the awful weather. My mood was dipping and I needed to get out and get some fresh air. Cabin fever. That's easy to write now, but it wasn't as easy to do then, when the grey clouds had metaphorically descended, as well as literally. I eventually dragged myself out of the house and down to the patch. On the walk down to the lake, the fine misty rain became more tenacious and I contemplated whether to turn back, when I heard someone say, 'Hello, Joe.' It was one of the new residents, a friendly chap who had recently started giving me 'goose updates' on the resident pair of Egyptian geese. 'I've been down, there's not much out there today,' he said to me with an air of certainty.

Should I even bother? I was there now, so a quick scan from the sheltered edge of the lake wouldn't go amiss. Bent up under a suitably sized branch, I trained my binoculars over the water. There she was. A stunning female smew, paddling compact and close to the water. An unexpected and unmistakable sawbill: slate-grey body, clean-white face and a chestnut-red head – gorgeous. I had to look a few times before I was suitably convinced, then I ran back to my car to fetch my scope.

Immeasurable excitement flooded over me with this discovery and my heart was pounding. All winter I'd secretly obsessed about finding a smew on the lake. Not only had I never seen a wild one, but like their close relations, goosander, I knew that during winter they could occasionally be found frequenting inland waterbodies. What a transformation, from feeling unmotivated to even go out, to being charged with an almost electric energy.

After the discovery of what was the first truly scarce species of bird there, my relationship with the patch began to change. It clearly had the potential to offer more than just common birds and so the frequency of my visits increased. I was aware that this could easily become an obsession and the more my relationship with the patch grew, the more disappointing it sometimes felt when a visit yielded little of note. I battled with a frustrating desire not to miss anything and this required sensible emotional regulation, balance and realism, so that I didn't find myself constantly wanting to go there.

These are some of the potential pitfalls when dedicating yourself to birdwatching in one exclusive area. Unless it's very close to where you live, then it's highly likely, given the frenetic nature of modern life, that you won't be able to visit as much as you might like. In the mind of somebody with depressive and obsessive tendencies, there can be some tough mental battles in order to regulate these kinds of feelings and to accept that life takes precedence. If you miss it – you miss it.

When I found it hard to break the cycle of obsessing over my patch, something I did, and would recommend to anyone, is to keep a gratitude journal. Every day I noted down the things that I was thankful for, so that if I was in a negative frame of mind, I could look back at the positives – no matter how small. I started to add things that were centred on birdwatching. I was thankful that I had access to the patch, that I lived reasonably close to it and that so much wildfowl wintered there. I was thankful that even if I couldn't visit as regularly as I wanted to, birds would always be there when I did. I shared the patch with them and their consistency brought me hope. It took a while to retrain my thoughts to this positive pattern, but that pattern is still there now. As is the keeping of a gratitude journal.

Away from all this purposeful searching and desire to discover exciting local birds, I find the greatest solace in just being outside. Standing, observing – breathing – picking up my scope and tripod and treading those well-trodden paths. The paths I know and love – my paths. Usually it's just me, and whilst this may not suit everybody it allows me to connect with where I am and, ultimately, connect more to myself and my feelings. Sometimes just looking out over the lake surface to the distantly whispering reeds can cleanse my mind after a troubling day, giving some escapism, relaxation and solitude. In my survey these were some of the key reasons that people gave for why they went birdwatching in the first place.

In a random hundred responses, words implying relaxation, such as 'calm', 'peaceful' and 'reflection', occurred twenty-seven times. Words associated with escapism, such as 'solitude', 'freedom' and 'away', were mentioned thirty-nine times, demonstrating that around a third of respondents feel that birdwatching gives them the space and time to reflect and relax. For me, having a place to go and disconnect has been a brilliant way to help relieve the symptoms of stress and anxiety – but how do these places actually help with that process?

I refer back to Dr William Bird's report, 'Natural Thinking', and specifically to where he wrote about the idea of 'restorative environments'. These are the places that are the most likely to help restore those who are fatigued from stress. He discusses the specific environmental features yielding these restorative qualities and there was an obvious correlation between these features and my patch. His list of restorative features reads as: 'verdant plants, calm or slow-moving water, spatial openness, park-like or savannah-like properties, unthreatening wildlife and sense of security'.[3]

Think of those outdoor places that you go to when you want to escape. I'm confident that most of them contain the majority, or at least one, of these features. It struck me just how many of the places I go birdwatching fulfil almost all elements of this list. Take Strumpshaw Fen RSPB reserve in Norfolk for example. Its website describes it as having the 'full range of Broadland habitats and wildlife', including 'reed beds, woodlands and orchid-rich meadows'.[4] The reserve also runs alongside one of Norfolk's arterial rivers, the Yare. A wildlife corridor of the finest order.

Strumpshaw Fen, with its rolling reed-bed views, definitely gets a tick for spatial openness. It also lends itself to savannah-like properties, in the sense that its vistas are expansive and are peppered with shrubs and trees. The blend of meadow, reed bed, wet carr and mixed woodland offers a wealth of verdant plants and the adjoining river and scattered wetlands provide calm or slow-moving water. The extensive range of flora and fauna is certainly unthreatening, and where else can you find a sense of belonging and security than in a place where everybody present shares a similar ethos and reason for being there?

My patch also meets Dr Bird's criteria for a restorative environment. It features open lawns of well-manicured grassland, richly skirted by scrubby bushes. The arboretum contains a lofty mix of mature trees, mainly firs but also a grand old cork oak. The largest lake is enclosed by alder trees, creating leaf-lined passageways on either bank. Wildlife is abundant throughout the park and the very fact that the land is private and residential gives a genuine sense of security.

The birdwatching locations considered as the best clearly offer much more than just the potential for birdwatchers to find and observe birds. Through their own natural and sometimes managed biodiversity, they also become environments for promoting restoration and recovery from stress. I posed a question on social media that related to this – what does a place need in order for it to be deemed as restorative? Most of the feedback followed a similar vein: peace, calmness and space to think, feel and absorb your surroundings.

From one hundred random survey responses, forty-three directly stated the place(s) that they most like to visit to go birdwatching. Of these forty-three responses, a large majority (thirty-four) named more than one location as their preferred location, with eighteen giving three or more. A vast range of habitats were mentioned within the responses, some examples being: rivers, woods, the coast, gardens, parks and numerous types of woodlands. The words 'variety', 'local' and 'multiple' occurred several times and the word 'patch' featured in four. Interestingly, twenty-five people mentioned the word 'reserve' or the names of specific reserves within their responses.

This shows that just over a third of respondents prefer to go birdwatching in multiple locations, and when the range of habitats mentioned is added to this, it's evident that the biodiversity and variety found in multiple locations offers a more enriching experience. Larger wildlife reserves tend naturally to contain a wider range of habitats, so they immediately offer this kind of experience too. It's perhaps no surprise then that birdwatchers choose to visit places that provide them the best opportunities to connect with nature and encounter a range of avifauna, thus enhancing their wellbeing.

Earlier I mentioned the work of the Kaplans on attention restoration. During their many years of research into the restorative properties of nature, they also set out some different criteria for restorative environments. These were: being away, extent, fascination and compatibility. These can also be applied to birdwatching locations, such as reserves, and again, to my patch. Being away is defined as 'somewhere that is a physically distinct location',[5] as birdwatching locations generally are; often they're extensive too, giving us the range and variety that we crave when seeking birds to observe. This all feeds into what fascinates us about the hobby and is what makes these places compatible with us.

The study poignantly states that, 'Restorative environments work best when one can settle into them, and when they provide enough to see, experience and think about to take up the available room in one's head.'[6] What a beautiful way of thinking about the places that you love, those places that you turn to for solace and comfort. Settling into an environment, as if it were a thick duvet on a winter's evening and absorbing their multi-sensory stimuli as they restore and rejuvenate us.

The last research from 'Natural Thinking' that I'll draw upon is from sociologist and academician Aaron Antonovsky, providing yet another set of criteria to apply to specific environments. His criteria create something he defines as a sense of coherence, meaning that a specific place has a structure that makes sense to us. He sets out three factors to make an environment coherent and they are: it's understandable, manageable and meaningful.[7] This can certainly be applied to nature reserves, as they're designed and managed in order to make sense to people. This reduces the complexity of a wild place, making it more accessible and ultimately helping us with stress-reduction.

Returning to my patch, it was early April and an event occurred that consolidated our bond. There had been a couple of ring ouzels reported around the Norfolk coast that week and deep inside I was longing to find one on the patch. Ring ouzels are a member of the thrush family, and are sometimes called the mountain blackbird. They breed in our uplands and migrate through our lowlands during spring and autumn passage. I felt more than just a longing to see one there though; it'd become an insatiable drive and determination for it to happen, something of an obsession.

In a spare twenty minutes, en route to a mindfulness session, I made a deliberate stop at the heathland that I'd appended to my patch. Near my parking spot was a hedge-lined horse paddock, providing a veritable haven for thrushes. As good a place as any to try and look for one. The heath is in a prime location; although fifteen miles inland from the Norfolk coast at Cromer, it's part of a sliver of woodland and heath stretching north-east from Norwich. This sandy-green artery makes the perfect stop-off point for anything migrating over the county, as it's the next obviously vegetated area in a southerly direction from the Holt–Cromer Ridge to the north.

My usual circuit had instilled a sense of serenity but hadn't yielded many birds. Then a blackbird appeared at the corner of the heath, next to the paddocks. As it moved along the fence line, it seemed to be carrying nesting material and I wondered where it was nesting. It turned to face me head-on, standing to attention as the sentinel of the hillside should. The nesting material was, in fact, a white-collar patch. Unmistakably I could now see – it was a ring ouzel.

My desire to see one of these proud birds had become reality. Excitement ensued, and I moved too quickly, flushing it into flight. It settled at the top of one of the trees lining the access track and uttered a harsh and guttural '*chack*' call from the highest branches. Up there it appeared even more commanding than when it'd stood tall earlier. Time seemed to stop, but in fact it'd flown by. I too had to fly as I was now late for my mindfulness session.

I hope you now have some idea of how beneficial and invigorating birdwatching at a local patch has been for me. As the seasons changed, so did the birds. And as the birds changed, I changed. The land changed around me and everything blended into a cycle of experience, in which I built a connection. I'd developed what could be described as a 'sense of place'.

A sense of place, in anthropological terms, is defined as the 'symbolic relationship formed by people, giving culturally shared emotional/affective meanings to a particular space or piece of land'.[8] This chimes strongly with the symbolism I had attached to my patch and, in fact, I'd originally named this chapter 'patch attachment' in early drafts. This symbolism grew with the more hours I spent there, the more species of birds I found, and the more profound enjoyment I experienced during and after my visits.

A study into sense of place by J. Cross identifies six categories of relationship that describe the ways people relate and connect to a place.[9] From these six, two stand out as particularly interesting. The first of these is a *commodified* relationship, and this links strongly to the selecting of a location to go birdwatching. This type of relationship with a place is about choosing and selecting it based on a list of desirable traits. Perhaps subconsciously these are the criteria for a restorative environment, the habitats in a particular area or even its historical bird records.

The second relationship is a *spiritual* one, one that's centred on emotions and feelings, chiefly; a sense of belonging. As the connection with a place grows and flourishes, alongside this comes a great sense of belonging there and of being a part of it. This is true of regularly visiting a place and unlocking its secrets, and welcoming this connection is vital for the promotion of positive feelings. It's this spiritual relationship that's become an integral part of my life. With every passing moment at my patch – every rustle in the breeze, every change in how it presents itself to me, every colour, sound, smell and scarce migrant bird – a new experience is brought to me. The more the connection grows and the magnetism increases, the more I feel at one with the world – physically, emotionally, spiritually and mentally.

The more I belong.

A few practical tips for birdwatching at a patch

Do your research and try to find somewhere that offers a range of habitats, increasing your chances of seeing more species of birds. This will only serve to enhance your enjoyment.

Explore everywhere and try to unearth those little alcoves and pockets of cover that could throw up something unexpected.

Work towards finding yourself a regular route that you can follow as this will enable you to develop solid and effective records.

Finally, enjoy it, absorb it and allow yourself to connect with it. The more you understand it, the more rewards you'll be able to reap from it.

VIII.

A sea-duck flotilla, flock unity and the march of the fieldfare

'One must maintain a little bit of summer, even in the middle of winter' – Henry David Thoreau

Winter. The frozen season. A time when days are short, and tempers are shorter. Low mood is rife and skies are dreary. I put pen to paper on this chapter just as the winter period was beginning and it really was a case of perfect timing. Although it can be a dark time, I find that thinking about winter conjures up great feelings of warmth, as it's a wondrous time for birdwatching. It's also synonymous with the sight of birds flocking together, described eloquently by a survey respondent as 'awe-inspiring and uplifting'.

In keeping with the pleasing visual aesthetics of birdwatching, winter flocks are often supplemented by glorious backdrops too. Rich, rouge sunsets with leafless trees standing spectral against them. Blankets of fog smothering ice-filled furrows. It's a shame that the beauty of these sometimes-colourless months can be lost on so many people. The outdoors and birdwatching can come as a welcome relief at a time that many perceive as visually austere. None more so than when the January sun breaks through that fog blanket and bathes all in a glowing reminder of the warmer months ahead.

Winter may be a great time for birdwatching, but it's not always a great time for people, and especially those of us who struggle with our mental health – particularly depression. Even those with little experience of mental health issues tend to be aware that the symptoms of depression can worsen during the winter months. These winter blues aren't just a notion, they're a proven phenomenon, recognised as a clinically diagnosable condition called Seasonal Affective Disorder, or SAD for short.

My mood is noticeably lower during winter, and when I first sought medical help with my mental health SAD was discussed and added to my 'list' of issues. This lowering of mood during winter is one of the most recognisable symptoms of SAD and other depressive symptoms such as lack of enjoyment, motivation and enthusiasm can also be apparent. This is believed to be a result of the shortening of daylight hours, causing a reduction in our exposure to natural sunlight.

This lack of natural light can affect certain hormone balances in the brain, which can then impact on our sleep patterns and overall mood. All the literature, leaflets and self-help guides on SAD give the same piece of advice. To try and get outdoors as much as possible during daylight hours and also to engage in low stress, exercise-based activities.

Sometimes in winter, it can just be a struggle to muster the motivation to leave the house and this is where your garden bird community can support you. Winter is a vital time to consistently provide them with nourishment, as in colder months it can be much harder for them to find food sources. It can also be harder for them to find sources of water, as they're often frozen over and inaccessible.

Therefore, it's important that you keep bird feeders well stocked and that you provide water in a shallow receptacle for drinking and bathing. Be sure to check that the water hasn't frozen and break any surface ice if you need to. Don't forget the ground-feeding bird species, such as dunnocks and blackbirds, although they will adapt to use hanging feeders if necessary. When it's snowy or icy, I leave a piece of wood out overnight and then lift it up in the morning to sprinkle some seed on the clear ground underneath. The ground-feeders always seem thankful.

In early 2018, vast swathes of the UK endured a week of intensive snowfall and sub-zero temperatures that was dubbed the 'beast from the east'. The sleepy Norfolk town where I live was snowed in completely. Cars found themselves rendered useless, as snowdrifts covered all the roads in and out of the conurbation. I could only get my nature fix on treacherous local walks, where finding a grip on the crystalline pavements was nothing short of a myth. But it felt good to be out and there seemed to be a noticeable increase of birds around the town.

On one of these walks, six bullfinches sat in a tree next to a driveway. Two houses down from them, a flighty redwing was nervously shifting around someone's front lawn. There were redwings and bullfinches in the cemetery too; in fact, both cemeteries were full of birds and it was all a bit surreal. Social media was awash with pictures of woodcocks and fieldfares in people's gardens, and to be honest, I was envious. I sliced some apples up in the hope of luring one into my own garden.

On the fourth day of snowfall, I stood by our sliding doors, ponderously looking out on to our back garden. I couldn't get to the patch, our road was now completely impassable, so a walk round town would have to suffice. Out of nowhere, a fieldfare was in the willow tree and another then appeared on the spindly hedge by the telephone exchange. This was a phenomenal visit for our small and enclosed outdoor space. They '*chacked*' and hacked about, brash and blundersome, before engaging in a spat with our resident blackbird. Then they flew off as quickly as they appeared, perhaps never to visit the garden again. In cold weather you never know what might be pushed into your local area, or even your garden, in search of sustenance.

One bird that can arrive on our shores in cold weather, often when their food crops fail in Nordic countries, are waxwings. There's someone who has a penchant for these unusual birds, and that's the enigmatic YOLOBirder. If you're not familiar with the name, YOLOBirder is a maverick bird and nature enthusiast, who in 2015 began to raise awareness about various bird-related causes, and about birds in general, through designing and producing a range of wonderful and funny T-shirts. I own rather a lot of these myself, including a brilliant waxwing-related one.

During the writing process, I occasionally suffered from bouts of writer's block, where I felt devoid of inspiration and motivation. During one of these periods, I took to social media to ask if anyone had any suggestions for chapter topics and one of the replies I got was 'birding in winter' – from none other than YOLOBirder. As he'd influenced its initial inception, I felt it was appropriate to ask if he would like to contribute and, of course, he was only ever going to write about waxwings. This was what he sent me:

Like many people, I tend to get a bit miserable and melancholy when the days are colder and the nights are drawing in. Getting outside can seem to require more effort, but the rewards are worth it. Flocks of redwing and fieldfare on the move, fields full of geese, but best of all, waxwings! The arrival of these beauties is something I look forward to every year and finding them is a guaranteed way to top up my feel-good tank. They look awesome: peachy plumage dabbed with yellow and red, hipster goatee, slicked-back quiff and a black bandit mask – making them look like some sort of exotic, avian supervillain. They make the most fantastic sound, like nothing else you'll hear, especially in larger groups. The best thing about them though, is their timing. Waxwings arrive from Scandinavia in winter – when I need them most. I think their collective noun should be a 'dose' of waxwings, because they're the best medicine for the winter blues.

As YOLO alluded to at the start of his response, you might feel frozen, both outside and in, but deep down you know that once you're outdoors there's always something natural to marvel at. In winter, nature really shows us its consistency, as no matter how cold it is outside, it continues its rhythmic cycle. Wrapped up in four, sometimes five layers to protect from the biting wind, you may be cocooned against the elements, yet you're still *living* them. It's the getting out there in the first place that can prove difficult and it can be so frustrating when the so-called 'black dog' stands there blocking the doorway.

But finally, I'd break down the barriers, get out of the house and go to my patch, feeling energised and positive. A stark contrast to my icy fingertips, fumbling numbly on optical focus wheels. My bird records also help to remind me that I've enjoyed a wealth of memorable birdwatching experiences during these darker times, a sentiment seemingly shared by others, when I sought the contents of a 'winter birdwatching checklist' on social media. I received a wealth of responses, sharing experiences much like my own. Flocks and fantastic spectacles seemed to be the main event, and where better to start than by sharing my own, most memorable winter birdwatching experience.

It was a day that sits 'mantle and scapular' above all others, and the scene was Titchwell Marsh RSPB reserve, in North Norfolk. Titchwell is widely regarded as one of the best nature reserves in the UK and it's also a place that meets the criteria for a restorative environment, as many reserves do. We're told, in an advertising strapline, that we can 'marvel at the big skies, stunning landscape and wonderful range of wildlife', and that's a description that I can't argue with.

The journey begins in a dusty car park, surrounded by dense foliage. In spring it's a good place to see and hear migrant warblers and a chorus of chiffchaff song is the usual backing track. Not in winter though, when it seems empty and quiet. From the north-west corner, a path snakes off through woodland and terminates at a visitor centre – a single-storey brick structure containing a shop, café and an all-important sightings board. Outside the rear of this is a range of well-stocked bird feeders, upon which the occasional brambling and redpoll can be seen.

From here, the main path cuts arterially north through some wet woodland, lined all the way by alder trees, a favoured haunt for flocks of winter finches. This acts as an arboreal edge to the famed salt marsh lying beyond, which is pockmarked with small saline pools that are often skirted by an array of wading birds. The path forks, with one leading off down the aptly named 'Meadow Trail', which also abuts an area of reed bed. The other path carries you onward to the sea, passing alongside two lagoons, one saltwater and the other fresh. The path then terminates at a somewhat paltry line of low-slung sand dunes. It was just beyond these sand dunes, on the beach itself, where my favourite winter birdwatching experience occurred.

Before we (I was with a friend) got that far we'd decided to have a bit of fun and do a day list. A day list is exactly what it sounds like: a list of birds seen, kept just for that day. As we walked out on to the main path, after some brief observations of the visitor centre bird feeders, we both heard the unmistakably urgent call of a firecrest. These boldly marked, angry-looking cousins of the goldcrest are always a treat to see, so to chance upon one so early in the day was wonderful. It moved through the foliage at eye level, leading us a merry dance and forever calling, before disappearing back into the foliage it had emerged from originally.

In the few weeks prior to our visit, social media had been awash, daily, with many epic treatises extolling the sea-duck 'spectacular' in the sheltered bay at Titchwell. Spectacular doesn't really do it justice, for the sight that unfolded just beyond the dune slacks was unforgettable. A few birdwatchers were gathered at the end of the path with their scopes trained on the sea and, as far as could be feasibly seen, the bay was brimming with flotillas of sea ducks, bobbing passively on the millpond-like water.

Birds were on the move all the time, with small groups taking off and moving east and west; a quintet of long-tailed ducks, in their beautifully demure winter coats, silently passed over a huge raft of black sea ducks – common scoters.

Further out, a few velvet scoters were mixed into flocks of their commoner relatives, picked out by the flash of white in their otherwise black wings. Closer in, a small group of goldeneyes paddled past, already practising their 'head-tossing' breeding display dances for the following spring.

It felt as though time had softly slowed to a state of inertia. Any negative thoughts had wafted away with the view and the only focus was the panorama of winter sea ducks in front of us. My friend wanted to record some video footage and, leaving him to his filming, I set up my scope and tripod to properly survey the scene and, in doing so, all the usual peripheral anxieties caused by work stress and overthinking were blocked out. The gentle lapping of wavelets a few feet away and the sound of the sea ducks' babbling contact calls were soothing me into an almost meditative state.

That state was broken by my friend shouting, 'Great northern diver!' – a bird I'd been hopeful of seeing, as several had been reported on the preceding days. He directed me to where it was taking off from and I got its hulking, torpedo-like frame into my scope view, which it nearly filled. It was a brute of a bird, its bulk akin to a jet taking off from a liquid runway, and it dominated all the other seabirds.

The sea-duck experience was hugely moving, but something even more so (in birdwatching terms) occurred shortly after. We went on, slightly inland, to the road leading to Choseley Barns, another well-known Norfolk birdwatching site and one of the few places left in the county to encounter corn buntings. These bulky birds can sometimes be heard from the telegraph wires that line the road, uttering their 'jangling keys' song. It's also a regular haunt for migratory groups of dotterel, known as 'trips', which also attract birdwatchers from far and wide, on their own trips to see them.

There had also been several unsubstantiated reports of a rough-legged buzzard in the fields south of the barns. Having never seen one myself, we stopped by to see if the reported bird was genuine. There was no sign of it on the side of the road where it was meant to be; however, on the other side, scattered across a field, was a gargantuan flock of pink-footed geese, or 'pinks', that my friend knew had been feeding in the area.

The lengthy observing of goose flocks is a birdwatching activity that's an acquired taste and not one that I find particularly enthusing. A few weeks earlier, my friend had taken me to spend some time with a large flock that were feeding in a field near his house. Within the flock he showed me how to identify tundra bean geese in amongst the vast number of pinks and I'd begun to enjoy the challenge of picking out their orange legs and bulkier frames. Patterns and puzzles.

We parked the car and began to watch the thousand-strong gaggle through our binoculars, standing next to another birdwatcher who was already scanning the flock with his scope. My friend asked him, 'Seen the Todd's?'

(Todd's Canada goose – a vagrant cousin of our feral ones.) In a northern lilt the man replied, 'No, but there's a red-breasted.' Being a novice goose watcher, this meant little to me, but the excitedly rushed reaction of my friend told me that this was a significant statement. After a quick look through the other birdwatcher's scope to confirm, our own scopes were erected and observation ensued.

We'd actually looked at one of these lurid geese before, in a wildfowl collection at Blakeney Harbour. Chestnut-red, charcoal-black and with vivid white flashes, it seemed far too exotic to be feeding in a Norfolk sugar-beet field, but the sighting was dutifully passed on to the birdwatching news services. After a short period of prolonged and undisturbed viewing, the arrival of two other birdwatchers served as our signal to leave. Whilst driving away, we discussed that heightened anticipation my friend had shown, and it transpired that not only had he not seen this species of goose in Norfolk before, but it was also the 300th species of bird he'd seen in the county.

Birdwatching is fascinating in its ability to transcend so many ranging feelings and thought processes. It was such a memorable winter's day, offering two completely contrasting experiences. From almost meditating at the sight of hundreds of sea ducks bobbing along, to being invigorated by the electrical energy of seeing a stupidly rare goose a few miles away. To share my friend's excitement was exhilarating for me too and was a stark parallel to the cotton-wool bubble of the sea ducks.

There's a running theme through many winter birdwatching experiences and that's the sheer numbers of birds. Call them what you want – flocks, groups, masses – one thing's for certain: there are lots of birds around in winter and generally, they like to stay together. This is somewhat paradoxical; that in some of our bleakest and loneliest times we can find comfort in the unity we see through nature.

Birds unite in winter for a number of reasons; simply put though, the more there are in a flock, then the more they can do. Multiple eyes to look for food, predators and shelter. Multiple bodies for warmth and comfort. Multiple birds for unity and collectiveness. In his letters on the parish of Selborne, Gilbert White commented on the wonder of birds flocking together in winter, saying that he couldn't help 'admiring these congregations' and that he felt their unity was driven by two great motives – love and hunger.[1]

He was right, there really is something extraordinary about a flock of birds. Their movements encapsulate freedom and fluidity, yet they always seem to stay symmetrically ordered as they flurry and whirl. Winter has its very own flock of birds, equipped with a seasonally appropriate name too – snow buntings. Many years ago, in my early days of birdwatching, I was at Salthouse on the North Norfolk coast with the friend who'd seen the red-breasted goose with me. We hoped that I'd see snow buntings for the first time.

It didn't take him long to locate the flock that had been frequenting the beach. Patiently shuffling along the shingle, making as little noise as possible, we found ourselves within a few metres of the feeding flock. There were thirty-five of these frosty finches, wearing rustic jackets over shirts of Arctic-white. Every now and then they'd take to the air together, up, uniformly, then down and on to their next feeding location. A bit like sand caught up in a sudden gust of wind, they were mesmerising in their movements.

Another type of bird that's redolent of winter is the thrush and you'll often see the term 'winter thrush flocks'. Our winter thrush flocks generally consist of two Scandinavian visitors, the redwing and the fieldfare, and large flocks will invariably contain a mixture of them both. Unsurprisingly, their names offer some identification tips; one tends to fare in fields and the other has red on its underwing. Fields, paddocks and grasslands are the best places to check for a flock and finding one is a great moment, as is connecting the nuanced names with the birds' appearance.

The heath was eerily quiet. It'd been a brisk walk around its dusty paths and I'd hoped to find a wintering warbler, but barely any birds were seen or heard. Following the downward slope to the copse enclosing the car park, I thought to myself, 'Why don't I have a brief look into the adjacent fields?' As someone who finds solitude in patterns and order, a treat for the eyes and mind awaited. Marching across the furrows in unison was a huge flock of fieldfares and redwings, ordered in lines of seemingly endless symmetry.

Their military gait and syncopated movements created an almost hypnotic sight. Stop. Start. Each bird scurried along, perhaps a foot in distance, then stood upright and proud with its wings projected behind it. This gave the birds a formal air, before they all bobbed down and ran again. In the depths of winter when fields are frosted over, and the sky is dark and brooding, these roving flocks move to wherever they can access their favoured feeding grounds of cropped grass. It's a great time to look for one.

As well as thrushes, winter is also one of the best times to see large flocks of finches. In the colder months, smaller groups of finches often coalesce with a larger assortment of species and the discovery of a large flock can be exciting as you sift through the different birds. Farmland is usually the best place to look for them, as many farmers allow their seed crops to turn over during the winter months, providing a fully stocked larder for seed-feeding birds.

Keep an eye out for 'set-aside strips', strips at the edges of fields which some farmers set aside for wildlife. These strips of seemingly dead foliage create fantastic wildlife corridors and are also a favoured haunt of finch flocks. I remember driving down a country lane in late December, somewhat lost. Suddenly, movement above the roadside verge caught my attention and revealed itself as the distinct shape of a reeling finch flock. I exited the car and watched them – still and silent – my binoculars following the flock as it wheeled around in unison. Safety in numbers.

There must have been hundreds of birds: greenfinches, goldfinches, linnets, yellowhammers and bramblings. Oh, bramblings! They're such a joy to behold, subtly beautiful and absolutely synonymous with the winter period. The colours of a cold dessert of vanilla ice-cream mixed with peach melba. The bramblings moved away from the other finches, flying from the field and up into the higher branches of a grand oak. I spent twenty minutes watching them and it was twenty minutes of contentment, reminding me of a comment from a survey respondent: 'Seeing flocks of birds helps me transcend any internal conflicts.'

There are a few other winter flocks to be documented in these pages and one of these is a flock that anyone, whether they have an interest in birds or not, can appreciate. It's a flock that captures our imaginations, can captivate a vast audience and can imprint itself in our memories. A true marvel of nature. A starling murmuration.

I stood on St Stephens Street in Norwich city centre, with dusk fast approaching. The darkness was folding inwards, compressed by the empty, low-rise office blocks that dominate this part of the city skyline. High-street stores were closing for the day, with A-boards being folded up and taken inside – it was the literal end of the meal deal. People were looking upwards, pointing, and my gaze followed their waggling fingers. What must have been several hundred starlings were wheeling around the indigo sky above. A solid mass that was morphing its shape in unison. A giant bulging sack of birds flattened out like the crest of a wave, then pulled and stretched as it seemed to inflate and deflate, adopting different outlines as it did.

These groupings, or murmurations, are thought to be a pre-roost ritual that acts as a signalling beacon for other starlings in the area. However the reality is that no one really knows why they do it. For a while, so many of us stood transfixed by the hypnotic patterns the birds were producing. I actually forgot I was on a city-centre shopping street and, for a moment, the concrete and glass melted away leaving just the raw and natural beauty of the starlings. Murmurations are often well documented locally, as well as being spread by word of mouth and social media. Look out for any local information and check one if you get the opportunity – you won't be disappointed.

Another aerial spectacle to behold is the roost flight and gathering of the corvid family; namely rooks, crows and jackdaws. Growing up only two villages and a short walk from one of Europe's biggest corvid roosts should've been symbolic, but I didn't realise it at the time. I lived near the great corvid roost at Buckenham Carr, in Norfolk's Mid-Yare Valley, and most evenings, in late autumn and winter, harsh and guttural '*caw*s' could be heard as a cloud of corvids passed overhead.

It was a tremendous sight, as thousands of birds flew home in a mesmerising ensemble of interloping blackness. A truly mindful birdwatching moment that as a child and teenager I never fully appreciated. As an adult, it felt significant for me to go back and watch the birds as they returned, so in late 2015, I did. As I stood absorbing the scene, I felt like a significant milestone in my own rediscovery had been reached. I had returned home, exactly as the rooks in the skies above me had.

Buckenham Marshes, where I had stood and watched them, is a tract of desolate marshland, managed by the RSPB. It's also a great location to look for winter raptors, from loping marsh harriers to pacey peregrines. Raptors, or birds of prey as they're also known, hold a prominent position in our human psyche and this was demonstrated through several survey responses. One in particular said that any raptor excited them and another stated that raptors were their favourite birds.

Perhaps the most poignant response came from someone writing how much they enjoyed watching birds of prey soaring as they felt they could relate to them. Maybe it's this freedom and majesty that makes them so symbolic. Perhaps it also lies in their strength and agility. They're the true monarchy of the bird world, regally representing some of the things that we also aspire to be.

I asked a fellow writer on the benefits of birdwatching, Paul Brook, if he'd like to share what he loves about birdwatching in winter; and everything that he wrote absolutely reinforces what I've written too. He mused about mixed flocks of birds and joyous visitors to his garden bird feeders – but it was this paragraph that shone through and which underpins this entire chapter. He said:

It's not always easy to find the energy or enthusiasm to get out birdwatching in the winter, but I'm always glad if I do. There's magic to be found in the winter birdwatching wonderland, whether that's a flushed woodcock, a roaming short-eared owl or a flock of winter thrushes or golden plovers. It helps that birds are generally easier to see in the winter – without leaves on the trees, woodland birdwatching is less demanding, and the boost to wildfowl numbers in the winter months means there's plenty to see on our wetlands.

I thank Paul for sharing this with me, and thus being able to share it with you.

Winter may be the season of discontent for many of us, but it's also a time when wonderful birdwatching experiences take place. Being outside should be savoured and enjoyed. It's a time to gorge our senses and stimulate positivity, through unforgettable moments and spectacles. Rapt in wonder and wrapped in layers, with both protecting us from frosty winds and icy thoughts. It's a season that, through sharing its own resilience with you, strengthens your own. It consolidates your respect for nature, connecting with you in positive, inspiring and uplifting ways. These can be dark times, but – when they're lit up by the flutter of wings and the flurry of a flock – in the season of discontent, often, I'm actually content.

A few practical tips about birdwatching in winter

If you find yourself of low mood in winter, getting outside and walking is great for overall wellbeing. Personally, I prefer being alone and immersing myself in my environment.

Find your own 'winter wonderland'. I wrote about my experience at Titchwell and it was mine that winter.

Scour your local area for flocks of birds such as tits, finches and thrushes. They make for enthralling viewing and occasionally contain rarer species.

Look out for roosts of birds such as raptors and corvids, and their pre-roost behaviour as they meet and fly in for the night. Also look out for news of any local starling murmurations as they're a winter spectacle not to be missed.

IX.

Hirundine flocks, spring passage and the warbler diaries

'O, wind, if winter comes, can spring be far behind?' –
Percy Bysshe Shelley

f winter is the season of discontent, then spring is the opposite. It's a time of re-emergence and reinvigoration, when starkness and darkness are replaced by an abundance of natural riches, all bathed in the glowing radiance of rising temperatures. Once-bare branches blossom and bud and their verdant leaves reach for their goal, the sun, with light and nourishment as their rewards.

During spring, shrub and scrub brim with warblers, who bring with them the soundtracks of the season of growth and life. The first arrival is the chiffchaff, a member of the *Phylloscopus* family, also known as the leaf warblers. These tireless tree-dwellers are all eye-stripes and melodies, but the chiffchaff delivers one of the simplest songs of the family – an onomatopoeic *'chiff-chaff-chiff-chaff'*. Stuttering and shuddering, it's the bugle call of spring, arriving in mid-March, although some birds overwinter in such glamorous locations as sewage treatment farms.

The first singing chiffchaff of the year heralds the arrival of lighter times. It's an urgent sound, shunting in the season with a piston pump of birdsong. It's a signal of change, not just in wildlife and weather, but for me in my outlook and overall mood too. As it returns in mid-March, it also acts as a portent of the vernal equinox. The lengthening of the daytime. The return of some sunshine into our lives.

Shortly after the return of the chiffchaffs then blackcaps start to arrive. They hail from a different family of warblers called *Sylvia*. The male birds are like sleek, silver bullets dipped in black ink, giving them the black caps of their name. The female birds appear to be less shiny and wear chestnut-red headgear, although they're no less beautiful than the males. They often begin their singing phrase with a scratchy and gritty ditty, which suddenly bursts into a rapid and fluted flurry of notes. It's a lovely sound, giving an uplifting and powerful feeling as it waltzes out of woodland scrub. As the blackcap's song springs forth from behind the hanging willow at my patch, I also spring up in mood, experiencing a different joy to the chiffchaff evocation.

Chiffchaffs show off. They edge their way up trees until they're in the highest reaches, which is where they always elect to sing from. However, blackcaps, like all other *Sylvia* warblers, are shyer birds. They secrete themselves within dense foliage, their presence only revealed by their sub-songs bubbling and scraping away. It requires more effort to locate one and maybe they enjoy this game of hide-and-seek, who knows? How joyous it is though, when their glossy frame flits on to a branch and sunlight catches them in full view, before they disappear again.

As chiffchaffs and blackcaps are rising in numbers, another *Phylloscopus* warbler shows up. Willow warblers superficially look much like chiffchaffs, although a fresh, young bird can seem an almost lemon-yellow. Their songs couldn't be any more different though. I'm repeating it in my mind as I write. I think it's seven notes, starting somewhere in mid-range with each one then tumbling down a flight of intonated stairs. There always seems to be fewer of these lovely singers around than any of the other spring warblers, which is a shame. Therefore, their song should be savoured even more.

The next three arrivals are also from the *Sylvia* family, although their songs are an altogether gravellier affair. Like their relations the blackcaps, they too reside in dense thickets and unlike the daintier *Phylloscopus* warblers they are solid and bulky, like all *Sylvia*. The first two to arrive are the whitethroats, common and lesser. Both reel off rough and disorderly songs, with the lesser ending theirs with a rattle of notes. Common whitethroats sing proud, from atop bushes and other lofty perches like telegraph wires. The lesser whitethroat is less bold and obtrusive, often singing from deep within a hedgerow and concealed from view.

Common whitethroats are yet another of those subtly striking birds and not only do they sing proud, but they stand proud too. Their buff belly clashes with their browner nape, whilst their rustic rufous wings contrast with dark-centred tertial feathers. Their name comes from their clean-white throat that leads up a grey-topped head. Lesser whitethroats are much demurer and are often described in identification guides as 'mouse-like'. They lack the rufous tones of their relatives and are an altogether smaller and more compact bird.

The whitethroats and their scraping melodies arrive in mid to late April. My first one at the patch in 2018 appeared on the nineteenth, a perfect example of the chronological consistency of nature and its wild but embedded calendar. This bird appeared at a time when my expectation to see one was beginning to become more acute. The timing felt right. For as long as their hawthorn outpost stands above their scrubland territory, there'll be a whitethroat. It's a glimmer of certainty in an uncertain world – a scratched signal of hope.

Another *Sylvia* warbler begins to sing towards the final days of April and early days of May and it's called the garden warbler. They're scarcely seen, and even when they are there's nothing obviously standout about them. You'd also be very lucky to see one in your garden, contrary to what their name might suggest. They appear to be a drab shade of brown, but when they're investigated more closely they show tints of olive and grey. Their song is as much of an enigma as their appearance: jauntily scratching before evolving into a fluted flurry, much like blackcaps, although never quite hitting the same levels of urgency. It's another lovely song that's awash with melodious qualities, whilst always remaining sandpaper-coarse, as is the *Sylvia* way.

This sonic schedule provides an uplifting accompaniment to a much-anticipated family of returning migrant birds, the *Hirundinidae* – or hirundines. Hirundine literally means 'of or resembling a swallow', and the (barn) swallow is the spearhead of these recurring springtime visitors. The earliest I've ever seen one return was on 2 April 2017, flying rapier-like over a woodland clearing at the patch. They're redolent of summer in the British countryside, nesting in barns and frequenting rural areas, perhaps one of our true farmland birds. There is an Ancient Greek saying that 'one swallow doesn't make a summer'. They almost certainly make a spring though.

Swallows are vibrant and rapid birds that bring a renewed energy to our springtime skies. Their vigour is infectious and seeing them back above, so pretty and purposeful, brings a smile and some reassurance; that they came back. Their angular shape, with pointed wings and a forked tail, cuts effortlessly through the air. Navy and black above, they're even richer in colour when the sun reflects off their glossy backs. Clean-white underneath and with a ruby-red throat and face, they '*chit*' and '*chip*' their way over sun-drenched paddocks and strafe low over fields and waterbodies, feeding on insects whilst they're on the wing.

Along with the swallows come their relatives, the martins, house and sand. Although a similar size, both lack the tail streamers that add such elegance to their cousins. The names of these two birds pertain to their choice of nesting habitat – houses and sandy banks. House martins are adorned with the same glossy blue-black topcoat as swallows, but are dazzlingly white underneath with a white rump patch. Sand martins seem to lack this cleanness, wearing an altogether 'dirtier' look. They also don't have a rump patch and are brown above, perhaps more in keeping with their preferred habitat.

In mid-May 2017, I visited the patch after work one day and found myself greeted by a captivating sight. A gigantic flock of hirundines were busy, feeding over the lake in the evening sun. Drifting, dipping, gliding and zipping – my rough count estimated well over a hundred birds. They seemed to be mainly swallows and house martins, although the occasional sand martin added a lighter shade to the darker tones of the other birds. I stood on the south-west corner of the lake, under the big alder tree, and found myself sinking into the hypnotic swirling of the flock.

The trance was broken by a slice. A scything slash through the cloud of birds. Arcing up high, it then dived back down through the flock, flying agile and level. It was my first swift of the year. Although superficially similar, the swift hails not from the *Hirundinidae* but from a different family of birds called the *Apodidae*. They're aerial scimitars. Blackened blades that cut through spring's blue skies. The arrival of swifts in our skyways marks the imminent arrival of British Summer Time and these magical mid-May migrators mark our summer out magnificently as they gleefully screech around our suburban streets in small groups.

May is also the peak time for listening to the dawn chorus. On still, fine mornings, as the sun rises, so do our birds. They sing to stake their territories and attract partners and will do this in every available hour of daylight. The larger ones tend to start first: blackbirds, thrushes and then robins. Later in the line-up comes the warblers and wrens, the size of the birds decreasing but definitely not the volume. It's a wonderful and enlightening experience to wake up with mellifluous birdsong all around you. It rises in intensity until it eventually envelopes everything. Try it for yourself and you won't be disappointed.

By early summer, our returning warblers will have all staked out their territories, with many having bedded down for the nesting season. They still sing though, and this brings great comfort to me, especially at the places I visit regularly. No matter how stressful or negative the day may have been, if I stop at my patch I know that a soothing chorus will be playing. In this season of renewal, I know that next to the sluice gate, where the sunken reeds lie under the overhang of the weeping willow, a blackcap will skulk and sing.

I know there'll be a chiffchaff, singing from a range of song posts as I walk down to the main lake. A meandering path to the right leads past the tangled tussock sedge that the whitethroat calls home. He can often be seen singing from the tops of this arid scrub and he reminds me of my own place in the world. Yes, life can feel impossible sometimes, maintaining who we are and what we do, but just stop and think about this bird. At the end of the summer months it will depart this thicket and embark on a 5000-kilometre journey to the Sahel region of Africa, south of the Sahara Desert.

What a momentous cross-continental trek, through arduous terrains and weather systems. A journey that overshadows our own worries and, in many ways, is a miracle of sorts. Yet he perches on his scrubby outpost, announcing his territory in gravelly tones; all whilst reminding me of who I really am in this world. These migrant birds act as markers, they're seasonal signposts that guide me around the patch. Like lighthouses, they help to map my life, but their beacon is their song, their territory and their presence.

Another signalman of spring is the cuckoo, an early-summer visitor that arrives from April and departs around September time. Listen out for their bubbly incantation any time you're near a tree-lined watercourse or body. These birds are also infamous for their parasitical egg-laying, in the nests of other birds, who then unwittingly raise the young cuckoo as their own. Long-tailed and clothed in jailbird stripes, cuckoos are a beautiful bird to behold.

When all of these springtime visitors coalesce, they make a wondrous sensory spectacle. Almost a year to the day that I'd observed the aforementioned hirundine flock, I felt the sudden urge after work to look again. It had been a day of meetings and visits, and after being confined to my car or indoors for most of it, I needed a little nature fix on the way home. A little bit of Bird Therapy.

The walk down to the lake offered the usual suspects: a warbling blackcap by the sluice and a chiffchaff atop the bare tree. On approaching the south-eastern side of the lake, I ambled past the whitethroat scrub and a scratch of song wafted over to me. I was home. As I stood between the two alders, the view opened out across the water and the hirundines were there yet again, like clockwork. The first to grasp my attention were the swifts, none of which had been present the previous week. A group of six cannoned around, twisting and chasing like aerial racing drivers. Hold on, there were more than six but gaining focus on them was tough. It took time to count them, but there were at least thirty birds.

There were swallows too and house martins, more than I'd seen together that spring; again there were around thirty birds in total. Scanning through them revealed none of their sandier cousins, but their bi-tonal, barrel-rolling frames still delighted me. As I watched them, a pedantic grumbling from the reed bed in front of me punctuated the air. It was a reed warbler, chattering away and sounding like the archaic sound of an old dial-up modem. Rhythmic and jittery, this is another essential sound of spring. These plain and pointed birds are members of the *Acrocephalus* warbler family – our reed-bed dwelling species. They also arrive in April and seem to appear in tandem with their cousins, sedge warblers.

In that moment – with the soaring flock above me, the warbler song at ground level, the blue sky, the glistening lake surface, the smooth air and the warm sun – I found myself struck by the grandeur of spring. It was one of those profound moments when everything else fades into insignificance. I was overawed by the beauty of the world around me. I was overawed by the power of nature.

During spring months, birds also pass through on migration in a movement known as 'spring passage'. This occurs again in autumn, in the opposite direction, as birds return from their northerly breeding grounds. There are patterns to be found in these movements, like when the ring ouzel arrived at my patch one April, then two years later almost to the day, three birds appeared in the exact same location. Gilbert White also wrote of a similar timely appearance of ring ouzels, as they passed through his parish of Selbourne in spring and autumn. He remarked on 'how punctual' they were[1], and he was accurate with his observation.

I vividly remember the uplifting experience of my first spring passage on the Norfolk coast. It was 12 April 2015, and I was spending the morning with my friend from the bird club. Our destination was Cley, a typical North Norfolk seaside village with a tall church, a shingle beach and a plethora of bird habitats. It's also a much-revered location for birdwatchers past and present and something of a birdwatchers' mecca. We were almost there, driving on the winding coast road and through the village of Salthouse. There had been easterly winds overnight, cloaking the morning in a fine drizzly mist that left a film of droplets on the car windscreen. We were both hoping that the weather might be secreting some grounded migrant birds nearby.

'Should we just check Gramborough Hill?' my friend asked.

'Why not, seeing as we're here.'

So, we headed towards the hill in question, which is actually a low-slung, cliff-like hummock lying to the eastern end of the Salthouse beach road. It's an easy place to look for birds, peppered with only a handful of bushes that I've been told aren't actually natural, but were planted by local birdwatchers in the hope of providing cover for tired migrants. The previous evening, a black redstart had been reported at dusk, flitting around on the top of the hill. It was a bird I'd never seen and I felt the rising excitement of possibly seeing a new, scarcer species.

A short walk across the crunching shingle took us through a sunken dip in the ground, then on to a grassy path with a wire fence running along it. My friend stopped suddenly as we reached the foot of the hill and remarked, 'Look at those wheatears.' My head swivelled to where he was looking, as wheatears were another bird on my list that I hoped to see that day. The previous weekend I'd trudged despondently around a few coastal sites on my own in the hope of seeing one but had drawn a blank. In truth, I didn't know what I was looking at half the time, a hopeless pitfall of those early days of birdwatching.

On the cropped turf of the field that lies adjacent to the hill stood ten of these proud passerines (the order of perching birds), seemingly glowing through the mist. They were striking to look at, all buff-pink and slate-grey. They stood tall, with their black and white tails pointing down to the ground; and the male birds' black eye-masks and white eye-stripes gave them an altogether mysterious look. The ten birds moved in unison, much like fieldfares do, although between posturing they ducked down, dart-like, before scuttling along to their next standing spot. Ten. After being so desperate to see just one.

Halfway up the hill proper, as we passed the lonely thickets, a dainty bird caught our eye as it flicked up, over the ridgeline and out of our view – beckoning us to follow. Sitting on the not-so-rocky outcrop and surveying the nearby waves was a female black redstart. She wasn't black though, she was a mousey shade of grey. Then her greyness, and that of the sky behind her, lit up as she revealed a bright orangey-red tail. We watched her for a while as she seemed to blend into sky and shingle, but her red tail served as yet another beacon of hope, shining, for the wonder of spring migration.

The day continued to bear avian gifts and all were new birds that I'd not seen before. Yellow and white wagtails on the 'Eye Field' at Cley; then later, a ring ouzel and a whinchat, further along the coast at West Runton, in some cliff-top paddocks. It's quite amusing to reflect on this day and the buzz of seeing these new species. Just the day before writing this, I was in central Norwich, shopping with my partner, and as we passed the Castle Mall we were persistently serenaded by a black redstart. Hundreds of shoppers were walking under this scarce singing bird, completely unaware of its presence, yet it'd been warbling above them for the entirety of the past month.

How funny, that on that day several years ago I travelled to the coast specifically to see a black redstart, yet yesterday I walked right under one in a city centre. In fact, every other bird I saw that day I've since encountered on my local patch and I've come to learn that migratory birds will stop off in many different places, to shelter and refuel.

Spring is winter's polar opposite. It's a microcosmic calendar of emergence and rejuvenation. Tiny buds, fresh blooms, scented air and emerging growth provide us with a sensory backdrop. It's the season of life itself, with vibrant flowers and birds acting as beacons to guide us. To lead us away from the relative darkness of winter and bring us new experiences and a renewed optimism. Then there are the sounds. The sweet and beautiful sounds, all around us, from sunrise to sunset. Trees and thickets become occupied territories, defended realms from which sweet melodies gush as we walk past on familiar paths.

If winter is the season of discontent, then spring is the opposite.

A few practical tips about birdwatching in spring

Enjoy the chronological return of your local warblers. Get to know the order in which they arrive and embrace the marvel of their migratory journey.

Watch your resident warblers as they preside over their territories and enjoy the wonder of their songs as they stake these out.

Try to find a local site where you can observe hirundines and their fantastic flight – waterbodies are great, as are fields and farmland.

Embrace the multi-sensory magic of spring. It's an absolute treat for the senses and beauty abounds, all around.

X.

The goldcrest crescendo, wind-flattened reeds and sixty pied flycatchers

'There is really no such thing as bad weather, only different kinds of good weather' – John Ruskin

As a birdwatcher, to keep records is a way of providing others with a window into our world. These compendiums of lists, notes, dates and times are so much more than just notebooks on nature; they're pages of memories. My own bird records act as a written gateway, opening to reveal the cherished imagery of special moments. Flicking open a page, I can see the names of fifteen bird species, written and catalogued in the order they were seen, but it's so much more than just a list. They're thought bubbles, floating on the page, each storing a special moment until they burst, releasing the sights, scents and feelings associated with that bird and place. One thing that these words always seem to invoke is the weather conditions on that day, for these are what create the backdrop of every experience.

When I read them, I'm reminded of the atmosphere of that exact moment. That atmosphere can be impacted by affective influences, such as mood and past experience, and it can also be affected by meteorological influences, such as temperature, air pressure, humidity and precipitation, or – as we might call it colloquially – the weather. The weather greatly impacts on birds, and therefore it impacts on the hobby of birdwatching. For example, in order for us to actually see them, many birds have to migrate here in the first place. They set off in favourable conditions but can't predict what they'll encounter on the way, meaning that occasionally they fall foul of the weather they fly into.

I'd heard tales of historic meteorological events, where the 'perfect' weather system for birdwatchers had formed off the Norfolk coast. Low pressure in the North Sea migratory passage, coupled with easterly/north-easterly winds blowing onshore, created a crosswind. A band of cloud cover and rainfall cutting across it meant that migrating birds essentially hit a 'wall' of weather leaving them with no choice but to drop down to land and find shelter, before continuing on their migratory journeys.

This phenomenon is known as a 'fall' of birds. A somewhat mythical occurrence in birdwatching and one that most people can only dream of. I read of one such fall, of thrushes, which alighted on the North Norfolk coast in October 2012. It was described as a cloud of birds that literally cascaded out of the sky in thousands. I wanted to find out more about these fabled falls and that's when I came across an article: 'The great immigration of early September 1965'.[1]

This unbelievable event happened all the way along the eastern seaboard of the UK. The conditions were perfect for a fall and it must have been sensational for anyone witnessing it. Some of the descriptions are ridiculous, regaling the sight of 'huge clouds of birds' in the sky and of two local people who had 'the extraordinary experience of redstarts descending from the mass of migrants overhead and alighting on their shoulders'. It's difficult to imagine what it must have felt like to have witnessed two great natural energies collide in mid-air above you; the potent discord of adverse weather conditions versus migratory birds and their innate need to move to fresh locations, causing it to literally rain with birds.

I knew it was unlikely I'd ever get to experience anything close to a fall. However, in August 2015, I found myself in the right place at exactly the right time. It was 23 August, a pivotal time during autumn bird migration, and I'd arranged to walk Blakeney Point to look for migrant birds with two of my birdwatching friends. I was lucky to be going with two veterans of this punishing four-mile journey down shingle and sandbank; I was in good and experienced company. A promising weather chart meant that we anticipated a decent enough day, but I don't think any of us had in mind what actually unfolded.

It seemed like it was going to be an arduous and unfruitful slog. There were no dark clouds descending and the breeze was weak at best. As far as the infamous Halfway House (actually just over a quarter of the total distance), we'd encountered little in the way of migrant birds, with just the odd whinchat to show for our efforts. Whilst checking the habitat there one of my friends got some grit in his eye, which stubbornly resisted several rinses and rubs. His frustration swelled and he almost turned around to walk back – then he spotted a pied flycatcher sitting out on a dense thicket of sea buckthorn.

The sight of a migrant bird seemed to renew his drive and energy and I can understand why. Seeing your first drift migrant in one of the UK's migratory hotspots is invigorating and looking at this monochromatic marvel, knowing it had travelled a long way to be sitting in front of us, filled me with satisfaction. Being somebody with a naturally low mood, I found it amazing how much positivity could be generated from a tiny moment. We soldiered on and began to see a few more birds – a whinchat here and a redstart there. We reached what is known as Near Point and entered into a dusty avenue lined by sea shrubs and shingle. This perpendicular gully felt like it should attract some migrant birds, appearing like a sandy landing strip, inviting us in to check it. It was here that the adrenaline started to kick in.

It began with a shout of 'I've got a wryneck' from nearby. My senses heightened as we honed in on where his binoculars were trained, and there it was, looking awkward and somewhat confused, at the base of a clump of *Suaeda*. We watched it for a while with its drab plumage camouflaging it expertly against the stony ground. Whilst we watched it, we were also being watched, by a redstart sitting on a nearby post.

Wrynecks are unusual birds, to say the least. They're members of the woodpecker family, but are seldom seen behaving like their tree-climbing cousins. Instead they can be found scuttling nervously on the ground, in search of their favoured food: ants. Their name is derived from the fact that they can turn their heads to a wry angle of nearly 180 degrees. They're also cryptically coloured in a mix of dull greys and browns, that when closely inspected create an intricately beautiful plumage pattern.

We walked on – periodically stopping and scanning around us. It had begun to drizzle, creating a misty haze that heralded the arrival of some heavier clouds. The wind had picked up a little too, flicking specks of drizzle on to our faces. Our optimism had crept up slightly, and you could sense it emanating from all three of us: could this be our moment? A shout of 'Harrier!' came from next to me; our binoculars whipped up to eye level and scanned the harbour, then, 'It's a Monties!' he exclaimed excitedly. Monties is the colloquial birdwatching name for the Montagu's harrier, the rarest breeding bird of prey in the UK, seldom seen and on that day, wholly unexpected.

Our anticipation had begun to snowball, fuelled by adrenaline, fatigue and sugary snacks. We ploughed on to Middle Point, leaving behind the three or so miles of shingle spit we'd searched already. Suddenly, the heavens opened and sheets of rain fell with renewed urgency, aggressively dowsing all in its path. In minutes we were soaked, exacerbated for me because of my naive lack of any waterproof clothing. The rain didn't bother us though as, truthfully, it was what we wanted, bringing a chance that our day could transform into something unimaginable. This fierce downpour seemed to be nucleated directly above us. Drenched, we looked at each other – and that's when it began.

The first recollection in my almost photographic memory of that day is a wheatear that was darting low along the shingle, between clumps of cover. The air above us was suddenly punctuated by the rasping '*speez*' calls of tree pipits as they passed overhead, their sound increasing in volume as the rain pushed them further down towards us. Then it happened. The fall. Suddenly every bush had sprung to life, becoming a moving carpet of shrubbery and avian wonderment.

What had earlier been a handful of birds seemed to rapidly escalate within a matter of seconds. A feathery deluge of migrant birds – wheatears, willow warblers and pied flycatchers – seemed to be spilling out before our eyes. They hid in any available herbaceous cover spread out between us and they strafed between clumps. The rain had rendered our binoculars unusable, but only eyes and mind were needed to absorb this breathtaking spectacle.

Moments like this require little in the way of words. A cursory sideways glance revealed the glow of wonder etched across all our faces, as we shared this awe-inspiring moment. We were in the midst of a good-sized fall of migrant birds, which had been grounded by the sudden burst of heavy rain, and everything I'd read and dreamed about was unfolding in front of me. The rain became so incessant that viewing conditions reached zero and we headed for some shelter at the side of a hut. We refuelled and uttered many words of astonishment at what we'd just witnessed. Wet through, but wild-eyed, we headed back.

As we embarked on the gruelling trek back down the shingle, we experienced not only a wheatear but also a pied flycatcher flying in off the sea. These were surreal moments for me, having only experienced blackbirds making land before. Watching a bird arrive, low and exhausted, on to our shores, helped me to complete the migration story in my mind. We discussed the multitude of birds we'd seen and we loosely agreed on (all approximations): fifty willow warblers, sixty pied flycatchers, twenty whinchats, ten redstarts, fifteen wheatears, and the aforementioned wryneck and Montagu's harrier.

These are the kinds of bird numbers that really are the subject of dreams, a true spectacle of the power of migration and the power of the weather. The feeling of inspiration that this experience imprinted on me lingered for days; actually, it lingers in my subconscious to this day. If anybody asks me what my best experience in birdwatching is, I always recount this story. To be honest, it's one of the most compelling and influential experiences of my adult life and one that I love to share and rekindle at any opportunity. It's been a privilege to share it in these pages too.

Later that year I experienced another fall, but this time it was just one species of bird and it was concentrated in one particular area. I'd been channelling my late-autumn birdwatching efforts into one place, Waxham, a quiet and often lonely location where other birdwatchers are seldom seen, bar the few hardy regulars. There's something in its solitude and emptiness that draws me there, especially in darker times. I visited there with my family often as a child and perhaps this is also why I've got an affinity with it as a restorative place.

The main area to look for birds at Waxham is the long belt of scrubby habitat that marches along the top of the sand dunes like a green army. It extends from the copse-like gardens of two holiday cottages and then runs south-east all the way to an area known as the 'pipe-dump', which borders a campsite. The pipe-dump is an industrial wasteland of rust-red pipes, left over from some offshore endeavour. The green vein that leads down to this is narrow and dense, making it easier to search for migrant birds. I would spend much more time there if I lived closer, but I don't, so it becomes my 'go-to' location during peak migration times.

Norfolk was experiencing ridiculously high numbers of goldcrest and on the coast, especially to the east, they were to be found in every tree and shrub. They formed a zipping, flitting and '*tseeing*' mass, which seemed to be everywhere, and on that day Waxham was no exception. There are certain segments of foliage along the dune edge that if you venture inside, you can often discover a wealth of hidden birds. Whilst deep in the muffled seclusion of one of these sections, I could hear a flock of goldcrests approaching me, their calls growing louder until I was completely immersed in them, counting upwards of sixty of these tiny birds as they passed round me on all sides.

The wonder of the wind isn't all about how it impacts bird migration; it also brings mindful moments through just its rawness. I was sitting on my own in the Fen Hide at Strumpshaw Fen RSPB once and my only company was the thirty-mile-per-hour crosswind that howled across the open reserve. The Fen Hide is an altogether rickety structure at best, and on a day of strong winds you can feel the walls literally shaking.

As the wind barrelled across the reed bed, every reed seemed to lay down flat as if ironed out. Between gusts, they sprung back to their usual erect position, only to be smoothed out by the next blow. The exhilarating blasts of cold, fresh air buffeted my mind, as well as the hide, disallowing any negative thoughts. A survey respondent made a delightful comment on the wind, saying that it 'helps to clear my mind of worries', a sentiment I connected with myself that day.

It was just as well that this hypnotic rippling effect was there for me to watch and enjoy as I hadn't seen a great deal of birds. I did notice a male marsh harrier, sitting out on a bare tree. He perched, still, as if he were the gatekeeper of the reed bed – seemingly unperturbed by the crosswinds blowing into him. His bright yellow legs gripped on to the wiry branches, and the smooth chestnut brown of his breast blended into a lighter head and small, sharp bill. I remembered that a survey respondent had written a lengthy passage about their own positive experience with marsh harriers, which I think is apt to share here:

> After a torrid few months last year (close bereavement, work stress, probable mid-life crisis) I felt a real, specific need to watch marsh harriers. We booked a holiday cottage in Suffolk and saw some great birds, but two or three days in I went off on my own and found a local reed bed that had breeding marsh harriers and sat there watching them for about an hour. Not something I'd experienced before but it felt like I was fulfilling a deep physiological need, a bit like drinking cool water after a long, dry day in the sun, and when I returned to the cottage my wife said that my face was 'shining' and I looked well for the first time in months.

I found this immensely thought-provoking. The respondent went on to describe the 'wildness' in a marsh harrier's eyes. What a beautiful way to epitomise its wildness, if its name didn't do so already. In fact, the places that you encounter them – the rolling reed beds that they call home – are the very embodiment of wildness. Ragged and unkempt, yet ordered and rigid – a paradox of the natural world.

Often the symptoms of depression are likened, proverbially, to a cloud, in a reference to the feeling of greyness hanging over everything. Thick, dark clouds can be the last thing anyone wants to see when they go outside or even look out through a window. However, cloud is to a birdwatcher what sun is to a bather. Clouds often mean rain. Rain is invigorating and cleansing and, if you're lucky, can lead to those much-revered 'fall' conditions. However, a fall doesn't need to be hundreds of birds; it can be just one or two.

After my first, unexpected encounter with a ring ouzel at my patch, I found myself regularly checking the heathland areas, in the hope of chancing upon other spring migrants. After yet another fruitless search I returned to my car, which was tucked away on the tree-lined access road, in a 'pull-in' next to the horse paddocks. As I got a metre from my car, a deluge of hail began to hammer down, rattling on my car's roof and bonnet like a drum roll on a tin can. I jumped the last step and got inside to get away from the pelting ice-bullets.

Once inside the confines of the car I went to switch my engine on to leave when a thought struck me – could this sudden downpour ground any migrant birds passing overhead? I figured it'd be worth a look and so I sat out the storm in the car for the next five minutes. Once it had subsided, the sun broke out sharply from behind the bulbous dark cloud that'd borne the hail, bathing all in a gleaming light that beckoned me to leave the car.

Just before I got out, I lifted my binoculars and had a quick scan of the paddocks. Was I dreaming? Along the hedgerow that formed the eastern boundary was a male ring ouzel, white-collared, scaly-winged and standing proud. This was fantastic! I decided I'd get a better view if I backtracked on to the heath and walked right over to the paddock fence, so I strolled over – ever purposeful. On the approach, I spied a small bright passerine flicking up on to one of the fence posts. Again, I lifted my binoculars to have a closer look, and was astounded to see that it was a male whinchat. He was buff and peachy and topped off with a sharp white supercilium. I'd only ever seen these migrant chats at the coast and couldn't believe my eyes (and luck). What a double act these two were, fantastic inland patch records that filled me with a great sense of pride and happiness.

Whilst exploring birdwatching in winter, I didn't really touch upon the wider impacts of winter weather on birds. In these frozen times, when the mind can also be metaphorically frozen, the cold can bring birds with it. It can also lead to warming moments like one that I experienced during a cold snap recently. Whenever it was possible, I'd check the local lakes for a rare winter visitor called the greater scaup. These diving ducks are much like a tufted duck, only larger, bottle-green in colour and lacking their titular tuft. The particular lake I was checking had previous winter records and I was hoping that one would drop by again on my watch.

This particular morning was very cold – ice cold. Everything was still dusted by an early-morning frost and the low temperature warranted the donning of gloves and several layers of clothing. I briskly walked to a spot where I could easily see the 'prize' lake, which was private but just about viewable. I was on my way to work; would it be worth the earlier start and braving the cold? I could immediately see that ice was covering most of the lake surface, except for a thin stretch no more than three metres wide by around ten long.

This had concentrated all the wildfowl into the iceless strip, which you'd have thought would make it easier to check, but the sheer number of ducks inside it was extraordinary. A massive grin spread across my face – this was awesome! What a great way to start my day! There were a number of species present, including two smart drake goosanders, but the undoubted highlight was the sheer number of tufted ducks. They were impossible to count as they constantly swirled and eddied, but I'd loosely estimate that two hundred 'tufties' were in this tiny channel. The ice-free area was acting like a beacon and must've been attracting birds usually resident at other local waterbodies.

On foggy mornings, I love to go down to my local patch for a walk even though I know that visibility will be limited. I may not see a lot in the way of birds, but there is something ethereal in being a part of the ghostly grey blanket laying over everything. There is a peaceful regality in the emergence of a china-white mute swan from a heavy cloud of fog, and great tranquillity in the distant silhouettes of dabbling ducks, tucked up in the lake fringes beneath the gloom.

The combination of mist and rain can be disorientating for birds, as we've seen from fall conditions. I was walking at the patch recently, under a heavy haze, when a powerful shower started all of a sudden. The weather was as confused as I was – the sun just didn't know whether to break out or hide. Rather than walk back to my car, I opted to take a brief look at the lake and this unearthed some interesting bird behaviour. The rain wasn't uncomfortable, it was satisfying. I could've sheltered but chose to stand out in the open with my hood up, embracing it.

On the lake surface, just inches above the water, several swallows were flying from left to right. They seemed only to move with each pump of their wings, creating a pulsing and rhythmic motion. Spread out across the lake were twenty or so birds, all following the same pattern, and we know how much I love a pattern. At the end of each cycle, they flew up high and back around to their starting point. It was a hypnotic sight and one that brings much wonder as I recall it now.

I've written of wind and rain, of falls of migratory birds, of blankets of fog and of layers of ice, but what about the weather of our summer months? I've spent many wonderful hours basking in the sun's warm glow whilst watching common terns fishing in the local lake. I've spent many hours crisscrossing local heaths in the blazing heat whilst waiting for a woodlark to ascend in glorious song flight.

Summer, though, is a time that's often bereft of avian activity. A time when migrant breeders are moving on to their second broods and when some are readying themselves for their vast migratory journeys ahead. One of the only constants in these times is the screeching of swifts as they cannon playfully through our streets. Wildfowl are seldom seen as they moult into their dowdy 'eclipse' plumages and during high summer I find my attentions transferring to another winged wonder, the butterfly.

Many a summer walk at my patch has been brightened up by a painted lady on the buddleia or a purple hairstreak atop the old oak tree. However, in a book about the therapeutic benefits of birds and not butterflies I'm not going to dwell on this as, who knows, it might make an interesting writing project one day. During a quiet time for birds though, a similar feeling of positivity can be found in these delicate dandies of the flower meadows.

A closing thought for when you're next outside – birdwatching, walking or just being – take stock and strip your mind back to the fundamentals. Allow yourself to become fully aware of your surroundings. Take a moment to appreciate what the weather is doing and how it influences your experience – how the air feels and how the light reflects off the surfaces around you. Inhale the earthy aroma of petrichor as dry ground is nourished by long-awaited raindrops. Listen to the droplets speed up as they break through the woodland canopy, dripping down from the topmost branches. We know that being outside is good for us and I'm an advocate for getting out, whatever the weather. As always, here are a few practical tips.

A few practical tips for enjoying the weather and exploring its relationship with birdwatching

Explore different places in different weather conditions as they alter your local avifauna.

Embrace and connect with the weather as part of your outdoor experiences. It can help to make you feel closer to nature, as it's all-encompassing.

It's almost impossible to predict, but if you ever experience a fall of birds – it's an unreal experience!

Keep an eye on your local waterbodies in winter as ice can concentrate large numbers of wildfowl into small areas.

XI.

Running with nature, sea-smoothed shingle and a miracle cure

'Step right up! It's the miracle cure we've all been waiting for' –
National Health Service

This quote is the strapline from the NHS webpage about the benefits of exercise.[1] A bold claim and one that I rubbished immediately, especially as I've always been careful to not claim birdwatching as any sort of 'cure'. However, it's then followed up by this: 'It can reduce your risk of major illnesses, such as heart disease, stroke, type 2 diabetes and cancer by up to 50% and lower your risk of early death by up to 30%.' OK, it's not a miracle cure, but those are some powerful statistics about our general health.

Further down the page was a sentence that leaped out at me: 'Research shows that physical activity can also boost self-esteem, mood, sleep quality and energy, as well as reducing your risk of stress, depression, dementia and Alzheimer's disease.' This was perfect as I'd been hopeful that our National Health Service would provide me with some strong words to assist my own. They hadn't let me down.

In the past few years we've seen large-scale initiatives, NHS and government-backed, extolling the importance of regular exercise and an active lifestyle. This has been driven home further by recent news of an obesity epidemic in the UK, particularly in children. Of all the five ways to well-birding, I guess that being active is the one that most people can relate to; if not because of its media coverage, then largely because it's common sense that an active lifestyle is good for you, both physically and mentally.

I like to think of myself as a fairly active person, in every sense of the word, although there are quite a few varied definitions in the *Oxford Dictionary*. As they link the most with my ideas about birdwatching, the two I'm going to use as a reference point here are: 'engaging or ready to engage in physically energetic pursuits' and '(of a person's mind or imagination) alert and lively'.[2]

I'll begin with a reflection on how physically active I actually am. Not much. I gave up smoking cigarettes nearly eight years ago, which has greatly improved my ability to engage with exercise. I still don't do enough of it though – far from it in fact. We're advised by the NHS that 'enough' is to aim for 150 minutes of physical activity a week, through a variety of activities. This activity should be strenuous enough that our breathing is harder and our heartbeat is faster than our resting rate, but we're still able to maintain a conversation.

The NHS webpage continued, telling us that we live in a sedentary world now more than we ever have done before. We spend an awful lot of time engrossed in gadgetry, whilst sitting or lying down. Apparently less of us work in manual labour jobs than in previous generations, and the advent of technology, intended to make our lives easier, has ultimately made us lazier. This inactivity and inertia can increase our chances of suffering from common and serious health complications. The end result is a massive strain on the NHS, costing up to ten billion pounds a year.

Birdwatching is a hugely active hobby. Why? Well I think it's fair to say that we often overlook the amount of activity we do whilst birdwatching. A lot of time is spent on foot, walking between viewing spots and vantage points, following familiar footpaths and trekking through a large variety of habitats – all usually in the name of finding birds. In fact, the best places to look for migrant birds are often at the end of lengthy walks to more rugged and inaccessible areas. I can vouch for the fact that walking the length of Blakeney Point or Burnham Overy Dunes and back is a serious physical (and mental) undertaking, but more often than not it's worth it.

My own physical activity – well, most of it – occurs whilst I'm birdwatching; and this activity is walking. Walking is good for you, we all know that, but have you ever considered why? I read a brilliant report entitled 'Walking Works', which collated evidence on the benefits of walking from a variety of sources. I was drawn to a small section titled 'Physical activity is good for our minds' that listed some of the positive benefits of walking for wellbeing.

It stated that, 'People that stay active get less stressed, sleep better, feel better, have a 30% lower risk of getting depressed and keep their minds sharp.'[3]

I tried to take up running, but the longest it ever lasted was six weeks. It required a time commitment that, personally, I struggled to stick with. One of the best things about it though was the fact that my running route passed a local mill, several streams, some lovely farmland and a small lake. This meant that every run was accompanied by birds; sometimes a skylark singing overhead, and once a grey heron, hunched under the bridge that the mill looms over. A lister, I thought to myself, would probably keep a 'whilst running list' wouldn't they? I didn't.

I became aware, through social media, of two birdwatchers who were also runners, and was keen to discuss their views on the two activities and how they interact. We got in touch and both were eager to share their experiences for this book. One of them began by stating that they'd had arguably some of their best and most memorable bird sightings whilst out running. I loved the process they shared, where they often had to retain identification features until they got home and then recall them, field guide in hand, to put a name to their observation.

They also spoke of similar responses to the natural environment to those that underpin the idea of Bird Therapy; the beneficial feelings associated with being alone, being in fresh air and immersing oneself in different landscapes. Their final paragraph opened with: 'Birds are also a great source of focus when the going gets tough, out on a run!' This is a sentiment that I strongly agree with, as I also use birds to help me regain focus, especially when I, too, find things tough in my life. I love the idea of using running therapeutically and naturally becoming immersed in another therapeutic activity at the same time.

A final note from this response is that, over time, they felt that their running had improved and were compelled to start entering competitive races. This more rigorous and structured approach to running could, they said, have had an adverse effect on their wellbeing, by adding the pressure to train more. One way they coped with that was to tune in with what was around them, listening to bird sounds and focusing on which bird was making them. They closed by saying: 'Before you know it, you're home, celebrating training or racing success, and relishing in the wildlife that's been around you the whole time that you never even realised was there under your nose. Awesome!'

I also spoke with Jonny Rankin, of Dove Step fame. If you're not familiar with Dove Step, it's the name of an initiative where Jonny undertakes endurance challenges, to raise funds for Operation Turtle Dove – a partner project that works to help these diminutive but enigmatic birds. Jonny says that he's an 'active' birdwatcher, describing his approach to the hobby as 'kinetic'. Whatever he's doing, he's birdwatching. Whether that's walking, cycling, running, commuting or even covering the entire length of Spain on foot as part of his charity work. He's always moving and he's always birdwatching.

He says that the avian rewards can vary, but having this daily approach has helped him to lower his expectations, with recent common tern and red kite sightings giving him what he describes as a 'high'. During the aforementioned Spanish sojourn, birds and watching them provided him with motivation and mental resolve during a gruelling 705-mile trek, across twenty-eight consecutive days. It was prolonged flight views of a great bustard, just north of Cáceres, that he felt had eased the enormity of the thirty miles he'd go on to cover that day.

For Jonny, birds are a pick-me-up, a focus and an obsession. Although he's keen to point out that he uses the word obsession cautiously, and he feels strongly that his hobby doesn't impact on his home and working life. Finding this kind of equilibrium is essential with any hobby, especially one as immersive as birdwatching. There's often a very thin line between a healthy pastime and an obsession. It's refreshing to hear that Jonny is aware of this and although he constantly watches and enjoys birds, it doesn't have a negative effect on him.

Finally, I spoke to Tristan Reid, whom I met through social media and who writes openly about his own battle with bipolar disorder. I knew that Tristan was a keen outdoor runner and was interested to hear his views on 'active birdwatching'. Firstly, he wanted to be clear that in the past he had been a 'very active birder and twitcher', but gave up due to his mental health, to the point that he no longer owns any optical equipment. Tristan and I had previously discussed the often-negative world of serious birdwatching and this came as no surprise to me.

He said that his engagement with wildlife was now more exercise-focused, with solace found in running in the Cumbrian fells, along Lakeland trails and on quiet country lanes. He stressed that the activity itself gave him the natural endorphin high associated with exercise, but that it also gave him time and space to engage with the natural environment. I was pleased to read that he took time to savour the broad variety of wildlife and the stunning views around him, sharing my own love of immersive multi-sensory environments.

I also revelled in his use of the phrase 'feeling part of the natural environment', another key component of my own views. I love the idea of a treaded connection with the land, and a feeling of whole-body immersion when absorbed in it. Tristan also said that it was this, combined with exercise, that gave him the mindfulness he desperately needed to help keep his mental health in balance. Through no prompting whatsoever, he again shared some of the key words that form Bird Therapy – mindfulness and balance – and it was wonderful that his thoughts connected with my own.

Engaging with physical activity whilst outdoors even has its own name, 'green exercise', a term coined by university professor and author Jules Pretty. He co-researched a journal article that asked what the 'best dose' of green exercise was for improving mental health.[4] It found that people who were sedentary and/or had poor mental wellbeing could benefit immediately from short bursts of regular physical activity in accessible green spaces. In context, a quick walk in a local park, or even doing some gardening, constitutes as green exercise. Now you have no excuse not to engage with your garden bird community.

In the conclusion, it found that outdoor time that was spent in the presence of water generated greater improvements in both self-esteem and mood. Every place I go birdwatching features water in some way, whether that's a lake, a wetland or a flooded field corner. Water is the star attraction of many birdwatching sites and if being active is even better for you when water is close by, then birdwatchers have struck a rich vein of wellness.

There are other benefits to be found in the environments that we birdwatch in. Benefits that we don't perhaps realise until we actually reflect on them. For example, the birds that people tend to want to see the most seem to turn up in far-flung locations, meaning that you often have to travel to see them and usually on foot. So, we birdwatchers often end up walking far and on a wide range of terrains, which all require different negotiation. This means that our bodies have to adapt and work harder to enable our steady passage.

I've never trekked on what could be considered as inhospitable terrain and, to be honest, I've barely left the UK. The arduous slog up Blakeney Point, however, is a test of stamina.

Late August 2017

The shingle crunched, spreading smoothly under my weight as my feet created hollow indentations. I found myself having to push down against the stones, my calf muscles straining with the exertion of foot against fluidity. An easterly wind had blown into the coastline overnight, inflating me with a sense of positivity for the long and punishing walk ahead. If I was lucky, it would bring with it the first migrant birds of August.

The majority of the walk yielded little of note, the swathes of *Suaeda* revealed only the resident birds – reed buntings, linnets and meadow pipits. Where were the warblers, chats and flycatchers? I knew that when I finally arrived at the fabled plantation there might be something hidden within its leaves, and this spurred me on. A long walk like this can be a lonely affair, but I find that I gain an opportunity for deep reflection. It's also a geographically fascinating and visually surreal location that naturally heightens your awareness.

As you head down to the tip of Blakeney Point, on your left lies salt marsh, tattooed with wet venous channels that are usually full of birds. On the right is the North Sea, running perpendicularly to the shingle spit, creating a tapered effect that feels like you're walking to the end of the earth. In the distance, the ground begins to undulate into a lunar landscape that cups its famous lifeboat house. On this building sits a curved roof and a squat observation tower, looking much like a blue barn, topped with a clean white trim. Or, as I envisage it, blue sea and white wave crests.

The salt marsh eventually opens out into the estuary of the River Glaven and the harbour at Morston. Rowing boats, small yachts and fishing vessels dot its surface, either floating on high water or resting placidly on the liquefied earth at low tide. Not only boats though; these shimmering mudflats gave me my first real taste of birds that day. A range of waders, feeding distantly on a raised bank. Seven different species, scuttling and probing as they fed.

I caught a glimpse of a harrier, a ringtail bird, a hen harrier? Possibly even a Montagu's or pallid, but it was hard to tell at such a distance. I watched until it flew out of view, then continued walking. Crunching, sliding and surfing on the shingle, up on to the rising dune system that rolls into the three 'points' and, further still, into the gully that held the wryneck two years ago. I could see the plantation appearing at the end of this tunnel. My target.

The plantation is shielded on one side by a slight ridge, which also provides grandstand seating. This tiered arrangement is the perfect place to indulge in some mindfulness practice – lying there, connecting with the land and calmly waiting. It's also a great place to stop for a refreshment break and so off came my rucksack and down I went, revelling in the softer ground and the relaxation of inertia. No sooner had I got some food out than I saw some movement in the foliage – and so the game began.

I sidled across a little to get closer to the source of the disturbance, lying back, the dry grass crunching around my ears. Head back and binoculars up – I waited and breathed. Inhaled, exhaled, and then out came a lemony willow warbler, quickly followed by another one chasing it. Then some movement flashed to my right, into one of the trees. I focused; yes, a female pied flycatcher – I'd found my migrants. Further right, I caught some more motion in my peripheral vision; it was a bird perching on a fence post. A whinchat, nervously flicking its tail and looking round with obvious anxiety. It flew quickly, over the ridge and away, just a fleeting moment spent together.

Lunch tasted good and the walk back seemed much less strenuous. Perhaps the mental by-product of a successful journey. No, I hadn't seen many birds and nothing particularly rare, but I'd had a wonderful afternoon in a stimulating and beautiful place, with actual time to think and feel, as well as to be active. What an inspiring combination, and all achieved in one single birdwatching visit.

There have been other occasions when I've looked for birds in terrains and habitats that haven't always been the easiest to traverse. I was recently at a local quarry that had been attracting some waders during autumn passage. And to check all of its prime water edges, I had to walk quite close to the existing quarry workings. My steps were delicate and cautious, as I knew the dangers of the sludgy ground, having seen a friend slide into it knee-deep a few weeks earlier. Wet terrain can be a similarly unruly surface, with bogs and marshes being fantastic habitats, but a nightmare to navigate. Care and attention are required at all times. Hyper-awareness.

We birdwatchers like to take our optics everywhere. In fact, I think Blakeney Point is one of the only places that I never see anyone carrying a scope and tripod, as that'd be foolish or perhaps foolhardy. Most of the time though, we lug our long lenses about with us, strapped to our backs or slung over our shoulders. A tripod, head and scope combination can weigh roughly five kilograms, which is a heavy load to carry round with you all day. Add to that a pair of binoculars slung around your neck and a backpack full of whatever else you need for a birdwatching session, and suddenly you're supporting quite a load.

As well as being a physically active pastime, birdwatching is also intensely mentally stimulating too. The Harvard University Medical School wrote some guidance on how to keep your mind sharp, suggesting six simple steps we can take to help improve and preserve our memory. The first two of these relate to Bird Therapy: to keep learning and to use all your senses. They state that 'the more senses you use in learning something, the more of your brain that will be involved in retaining the memory.'[5] Therefore birdwatching, as a fully sensory experience, utilises our brain power.

The part of the brain that deals with memory is called the hippocampus, and it's one of the first areas damaged by Alzheimer's disease. An NHS article, simply titled 'Keep your brain active',[6] featured an Australian study into whether keeping your mind active can help to prevent age-related shrinking of the hippocampus. Whilst the study was small and the results perhaps not fully conclusive, it did find that a 'high level of complex mental activity' throughout life, akin to 'lifelong learning', could be linked to a lower rate of hippocampal atrophy.

So, learning throughout life can be good for your brain and engagement in hobbies promotes this, so are hobbies good for you generally? Research actually suggests that one of the best ways to keep the mind 'sharp' or 'active' is to start a new hobby. A study by Denise C. Park et al.[7] explored whether starting a new hobby, to learn specific skills over a three-month period, could enhance brain function in older adults. The hobbies studied were quilting and digital photography, and evidence was found that productive engagement in demanding, everyday tasks improves memory function.

Finally, I looked at a study by Diana Bowler et al.,[8] considering a perspective that nature and outdoor environments don't actually have a specific benefit for health and wellbeing; rather that they promote and encourage healthy behaviour and activity. I suppose this makes sense. When you're outside, you're away from the distractions of modern life such as technology and social media and when away from our lounges and laptops, we're more likely to partake in activities or behaviours that have a direct correlation to the environment we're immersed in. So, if you're spending time in a woodland environment, you're much more likely to be observing woodland wildlife than watching television! This is very much in line with the idea of 'being away', one of the Kaplans' criteria for a restorative environment. It also reminded me of a phrase I coined, for a chapter that I never wrote – 'disconnect to connect'.

It's evident that birdwatching is an active hobby and that this occurs on many different levels. It gets you outside and exerting, both physically and mentally, in environments that are proven to be good for your overall wellbeing. It ticks all the metaphorical boxes, even if you've never realised it before. Mentally, the processes and experiences of learning through birdwatching are ongoing, lifelong even, and provide a plethora of excellent ways to keep your mind active. What's not to love?

Some practical tips about being active through birdwatching

Try to vary the habitats and terrain you birdwatch in; it can be good for keeping you active and alert.

Embrace the elements whilst exercising, so they become a natural part of your fitness routine.

Try and be active close to water as it's purported to be better for your wellbeing; also try to exercise outdoors if you can.

Birdwatching keeps your mind active as well as your body; embrace every moment you spend outside for the holistically positive experience that it is.

XII.

Bramble patches, a garden warbler and learning through experience

'Experience is simply the name we give our mistakes' – Oscar Wilde

earning is good for mental wellbeing is the line taken by the NHS in their online guidance on the five ways to wellbeing. They report that people who engage in 'lifelong' learning, those who continue to learn beyond compulsory education and throughout life, may experience all manner of positive effects. These include greater satisfaction, optimism and ability to cope with stress. They also state that, 'Learning can boost confidence and self-esteem, help build a sense of purpose, and help us connect with others.'[1] Does any of that seem familiar?

Learning can be defined as the process of taking information in, processing it, storing it and then being able to recall it later. I've shared many birdwatching experiences with you in these pages and, when broken down, these could be considered as the component parts of a similar, developmental journey. Observe bird, identify bird, remember and recall it. More pertinent perhaps is that throughout this process I've been continually learning about myself and reflecting on my feelings and thoughts, as is such a vital part of the learning process.

In order for us to learn there has to be some kind of catalyst. My own catalysts for learning about birds were my breakdown, that buzzard and a childhood spent in my beloved Broadland. The more I reflected, the more I realised just how much of a true learning experience birdwatching is. I knew that I would be writing about it as part of my five ways to well-birding, but when I realised just how many teaching and learning theories correlated with birdwatching I found myself to be surprised and excited to explore the topic.

Whilst studying for my professional teaching qualification, I had to research a wide range of educational theories. One of my favourites was the experiential learning cycle, first described by David Kolb. Not only do I utilise it in my own teaching but it also applies wonderfully to birdwatching too. The principle of this cycle is that we experience something (Kolb calls this 'concrete experience'), reflect on it ('reflect on experience'), develop our own methods of understanding it ('abstract conceptualisation') and then test these methods out in a similar experience ('plan active experimentation'), thus creating a cycle.[2]

Every birdwatching observation is a new concrete experience which we then invariably reflect on in some way. It may be close, distant or obscured. It may be in the form of some scribbled notes, or perhaps a photograph. Whatever form it takes, it leads us to some type of reflection. It's the same with birdsongs and calls, which when written in a guidebook can appear very odd. Yet when a grey wagtail flies overhead, calling, you know that it's grey and not pied because you've experienced and memorised the nuance in the sound and mentally annotated it for future reference.

I vividly remember the first time I saw, and subsequently identified, a garden warbler by myself. I watched this nondescript and skulking warbler for nearly ten minutes before I started to connect the dots. What struck me was how plain it was to look at, as most birds have at least one distinguishing feature to help narrow down an identification. It could be feather streaking, bill colour or perhaps an eye-ring; but then I realised that was the point – the identification feature I was looking for was actually the fact that there wasn't one!

I noted its plainness, but also the fact that it had a gentle look to it, appearing friendly, if a bird can appear so. I knew I had a basic bird guide back in my car, so strolled back to get it and see if I could deduce the identity of this puzzling bird. I knew that the passerines were towards the back of the book, so swiftly leafed through, passing the robin and reed warbler before alighting upon a garden warbler. Yes, this was the bird I was searching for, affirmed further by the words nondescript, skulking and gentle within its description.

From a concrete experience in seeing the bird, I'd reflected on what I'd seen and settled on an identification. I took these features and developed my own abstract concept for remembering the identification features of a garden warbler, meaning that the next time I was out, if I saw a mousey-grey warbler from the *Sylvia* genus, I'd be able to recognise it as one. This forms an ongoing cycle of experiential learning that occurs whenever you go birdwatching, whether you're consciously aware of it or not.

The use of a field guide for assistance here is also notable. I read a fascinating study into field guides and listing that was featured in a journal named *Human Studies*.[3] What I found so refreshing about this research was that the two authors, John Law and Michael Lynch, resided in the UK and America respectively, giving us representation from the two main birdwatching nations of the world.

In a section on field guides, they dissected the presentation and layout of several and considered what made them effective, or not. A good field guide had to be realistic in its descriptions for ease of use in the field. It had to appeal to both the audio and visual senses, containing notes on the way a bird both looks and sounds. Illustrations were a requisite – as was the strategic use of captions and descriptions. This combination of words and pictures can help us to create our own abstract conceptualisations.

In conclusion, they argued that field guides 'provide a descriptive organization to the craft of seeing species in the field'. They act as a backup for our instincts and a consolidator for our conceptualisation. In some ways, a good field guide can become a birdwatcher's 'bible', and I strongly recommend using one, as it adds an extra dimension to your experiences with birds. I personally use, and would recommend to UK birdwatchers, the *Collins Bird Guide*, as it features all of the traits recognised in the study. However, there are a range of other excellent titles out there, so be sure to have a look through a few before committing to one.

Many of my outdoor experiences have had a profound effect on me and my wellbeing, and this sets me up nicely for the next element of learning that I've found to be prevalent in birdwatching – the affective domain. You may have encountered Bloom's taxonomy before. If not, it's an educational model that outlines a 'hierarchy of cognitive-learning levels, ranging from basic knowledge through to advanced evaluation'. As part of this model, Dr Benjamin Bloom weaved in his own 'domains of learning'. He named one of these the 'affective' domain, and it focused on emotions, values and attitudes.[4]

Time spent alone, in beautiful surroundings, with only nature for company and birds to focus on, has caused my overall attitude towards life to shift. I don't have to try when I'm outdoors and I don't have to attempt to please anyone or try to be accepted. The more time I spent with myself, the more I accepted the changes I was making in my life and I also learned that I could enjoy my own company again. My mind could settle into the calming and restorative environments that I was engaging in, helping me to take a more measured approach to my actions and decisions, and slowing down my ever-frenetic brain.

In learning, repetition helps to embed something into the memory. I stand by my initial decision to focus on this, by embedding my basic birdwatching skills and learning about the common bird species first. I began this process visually, before moving on to calls and songs, always focusing on familiar environments and the decoding of their avian inhabitants. After a while I expanded my parameters and spent some time at coastal sites, visiting flagship reserves and hunting for migrant birds in peak conditions. It was a process much like the building of a wall. I laid the foundations and then built up each layer of knowledge through experience and contact.

When you repeatedly visit the same places and observe the same species of birds, you develop your own memory bank of how each bird looks and behaves. In birdwatching, this 'feel' for a bird has its own name – 'jizz' – an unusual term that basically means the general impression and character of a bird that distinguishes it from another. The idea of recognising a bird's jizz is innate to each observer's perception of a bird. Often when I'm out birdwatching with someone else, they'll be able to identify something flying overhead or in the distance with just the naked eye. I'll ask them how they did it and they'll invariably reply that they 'just can'. When observing a bird at a distance you have to look at the whole picture of the bird and features such as flight style, posture and build. So, here's an example.

A small bird flits out of the willow in my garden and down on to the bird feeders. I'm watching from the dinner table, from around seven metres away, through glass and without binoculars. It's definitely a tit, as it has yellow underparts and a blueish tinge to its uppers. It turns slightly and I can see that it has a more green-grey sheen to its wings, with a white bar running down it. It's bigger than a blue tit, bulkier and less delicate in its movements. Its breast is split by a black hourglass-shaped pattern and a black crown sits on bright white cheeks, like an Everton mint. I know it's larger than a blue tit or a coal tit, and I weigh up the combination of distinguishing features, concluding that it's a great tit. It was all in the general feel of it – its jizz.

As birdwatching mainly takes place outdoors, I have to take a look at the wider concept of outdoor learning. The Institute for Outdoor Learning describes outdoor learning experiences as a 'stimulating source of fascination [and] personal growth'.[5] Birdwatching is, without question, a stimulating and fascinating activity that promotes personal growth – whether that's in managing one's own mental wellbeing, or in developing new social relationships and interactions. My greatest personal growth has been in gaining a deeper understanding and connection with my local area and the environment in general. Let me elaborate.

I love to mentally explore a map, to try and seek out new nature sites, and when I see my surroundings laid out in front of me, ordered in a grid, I feel safe and reassured. My eyes are drawn to blue and green smudges and blotches, representing open water, woods and grassland. I love the thrill and anticipation that each prospective new site brings with it and the even greater thrill of visiting sites for the first time, exploring them and unlocking their potential.

On a map, these smudges are nothing but blocks of two-dimensional colour, but on the ground and in the field, they transform as they become three-dimensional. Each of these areas is a pocket of habitat, a source of life, which will invariably contain several smaller and concentrated habitats. A perfect example of this is the humble bramble patch, usually found alongside a country lane or deep within a shaded woodland.

Smothered in shafts of sunlight and residing in darkened glades, if you look closer into the thorns and fruits, you'll begin to see the dazzling array of life that one plant can support. Bees busy collecting pollen, hoverflies loafing, butterflies supping nectar. Focus, and on a warm day you'll see lots of other flying insects too. Look down – there'll be ants, spiders and beetles around your feet. Avert your eyes to the canopy above. A family of blue tits might be busy roving through, led by their inquisitive and yellow-washed young. A wood pigeon looks on – bemused or confused, it's impossible to tell. These are the many layers of nature, just waiting to be unpeeled.

Whilst out birdwatching, you may also become aware of other types of wildlife. Perhaps this is why many birdwatchers branch out into other fields of natural history? Through my own time spent birdwatching, I'm now interested in butterflies, orchids and, to some extent, moths. I'm sure that I wouldn't have taken an interest in these, were it not for encountering them in the species-rich areas I visit, or from spending time with other likeminded people.

The way that nature is intertwined with life itself becomes clearer the more time you spend immersed in it. These are the true connections and you soon come to realise that you're just an inconsequential part of this system. No matter how bad you think things are, your connections within nature are strong, tangible and ever-present. My nucleated approach coincided with feelings of balance and stability in my life. If I felt I needed reassurance and comfort, I stayed local and used familiar sites as my safety net. I enjoyed my forays outside of my comfort zone and loved to visit new places with different people, but I always felt the magnetic pull of the places I know and love.

I've learned and accepted that we're connected.

Some practical tips about learning through birdwatching

Learning is proven to be good for wellbeing and can be facilitated by starting a new hobby, like birdwatching.

Experience is a great way to learn and birdwatching is full of experiences – embrace them! Also embrace repetition. Watch the same bird, visit the same site again. It helps to deepen and embed learning.

Pick your field guide wisely – it's your birdwatching bible.

Explore and continue to explore – it's the best way to discover new things. Take notice of the new things you encounter whilst birdwatching, it may spark another interest.

XIII.

An evolving hobby, a return to the heath and going back to basics

As April showers spit and slow, they wet the barren heath.
The gloomy clouds roll darker so an oak I stand beneath.
A broken shaft, the archer's bow, arcs over, sharp and true.
The pot of gold is this place of old, a land that's part of you.

There's a recurring theme throughout these pages and it's this that draws them to a close. I like to think of it as a tangled understory that's grown in unison with the book, with chapter one as the roots of my journey and this final chapter as the flowers and fruits of my labours – pertinent, then, that I'm writing about growth. The growth of ideas and feelings, the growth of me as a person, the growth of Bird Therapy and the growth of the changes that have happened throughout my exploration of the therapeutic benefits of birdwatching.

Birds and nature are my anchor to the present. They're constant and reliable, in a way that people rarely are, perhaps a reason why I and many others turn to them at times when nothing else seems to help. Even when the world around us is a dark place, the birds still sing, they still migrate – they're just there, being, in a way that perhaps we all aspire to be ourselves. A survey respondent rightfully stated that they 'can never let me down. If I don't see a bird it's not their fault, it's because I didn't see anything.'

All around us, things are constantly changing. The weather, the world, society and us. Change is a feature of life, no matter how big or small. I began writing this chapter, somewhat ironically, at a time of great change in my life. My mental health was stable enough for me to feel confident in changing jobs and this is something that's always been a great challenge for me. I lay strong and deep roots wherever I plant myself and find it incredibly difficult to shake the soil off if I uproot.

I never claim that birdwatching is solely responsible for my current mental stability as there are many other influencing factors, but it's certainly helped me to achieve a semblance of balance. It's assisted me in myriad ways, as I've tried to explore and demonstrate in these pages. I've endeavoured to take you on this progressive journey with me – meandering and discovering – like a watercourse of wellbeing on a winding journey to a sea of tranquillity.

My OCD has led to many retakes of this book in a process I described on my blog as: 'Type. Delete. Type. Repeat... for hours and hours. Get angry. Stop writing. Freak out. Go for a walk. Give up.' I've had to be acutely aware of how much of *me* I've committed to this book. I'm forever conscious of its propensity to break me and of that rising sickness when hundreds of words jumble into incoherence; the fear that it'll never be good enough.

Through the years of writing, I tried to sample as many different approaches to birdwatching as I could, within the parameters of work and life. Through not imposing a strict timescale on this, I've been able to spend some time reflecting and analysing my experiences with the different approaches I've tried. The most powerful was the entire year I spent stoically building my relationship with and understanding of a single site, my patch. What a wonderful and insightful year it turned out to be. My affinity with that place grew strong and meaningful and I really felt like it evolved into a spiritual connection with the land, which was something I'd not experienced before.

The friend whose patch was Sparham Pools had to take some time away, thus leaving this inviting site unwatched, in what was a birdwatching travesty of epic proportions. It was still close to home and I knew it well, so perhaps I could treat it as a personal experiment on how it would feel to change patches? I felt torn. Could I really leave my beloved patch behind and move on to another place? Would it feel the same? Would it have a similar calming effect on me?

A new year at a new patch and it was sluggishly dragging its heels, like a petulant child. Within a few weeks, I'd quickly totted up the common bird species I'd expected to see, but it had already started to develop a sense of monotony. My mood lifted in mid-January, with the appearance of a great grey shrike. Shrikes are the gangsters of the avian world, cunning predators and beautifully marked. They're a smoky-blue, silvery-grey colour on top and clean-white underneath, wearing a black mask and wing. Although not a large bird, being a similar size to a fieldfare, they appear stocky and powerful as they perch in their usual spots in the tops of trees or hedgerows.

It didn't take long for an air of negativity to set in again though, as I didn't see any new species of bird for a few months. I began to feel like I wasn't quite connecting with the site as I'd hoped and I began to wonder why. Why wasn't I connecting with it? I felt like the patch met the criteria for a restorative environment; admittedly, it lacked in spatial openness, but it wasn't that. I was struggling to put my finger on precisely what it was that made it feel less like a second home – like a safe place to escape to.

I wondered whether it might be its geographical location – but then I realised that it was actually in a more logical and accessible position, being directly on my journey home from work. Perhaps that was part of the issue? The fact that I could drive past and check around it really easily, possibly weakening any feelings of awe and wonder. Perhaps it was my new walking routes that had my mind wandering? The crux of the walk was circular and relatively well enclosed by trees and vegetation, and the steep sides of the old pit meant that I was always looking down to the waterline.

I never felt like I was close enough to any wildfowl or water birds that were present, like the ornately coloured drake mandarin duck that I chanced upon one afternoon. However vibrant he may have been, he was always a distant splash of colour that was only viewable through a scope. It seems fitting, then, that one of the only places where I felt truly at ease was the one where I could be level with and attuned to the avifauna. A rickety descent down an old set of wooden steps would lead me on to a surprisingly stable fisherman's float at the water's edge. I may not have been any closer, but I felt as though I was, and it's feelings that matter to me, as you know by now.

At the eastern edge of the pit sat four private fishing lakes that for many years I'd tried to gain access to, but to no avail, eventually settling for just long-range observations. Some scarcer birds had been seen on these pits by myself and others, including goosanders, scaups, black terns and Arctic terns, to name but a few; I found it frustrating that I couldn't respectfully walk around them to explore and connect. Was it this lack of overall access that was impacting on my experience? After all, birds are symbolic of freedom and movement and surely it was paradoxical to be restricted in my own engagement with them. However, I do accept that this is an element of my hobby beyond my control and there will always be places that are out of reach.

I've got absolutely no issue with sharing outdoor spaces with other people – whether that's birdwatchers, dog walkers or general outdoor recreationists. I always take the time to converse with people I meet and I truly believe that it's vital we engage, explore, educate and enrich our lives through the outdoors and through nature. However I think, rather selfishly, that for me to develop a true sense of place, I have to experience it on my own as much as possible.

I did have a lot of time to myself there but it wasn't like my old patch. My old patch felt like my own little world – my microcosm – my haven. Here just didn't. You may recall that one of the criteria for a restorative environment was to have spatial openness. I feel that spatial openness also relates to our mental space. It creates that state of being away, of feeling free and decompressed. Perhaps we need our mental spatial openness just as much?

I also annexed several satellite sites to the main area of the pools. This was to offset the banality of the circular walk and to try and increase the biodiversity of habitats. They were all interconnected and ran along a section of the river valley. In fact, the whole labyrinthine network would've been walkable if it hadn't been compartmentalised by various landowners. This meant I had to return to my car to move on to the next starting point, and this was yet another reason why the new patch didn't inspire me as much as the old one. It just wasn't the way that my birdwatching experiences were supposed to unfold. In this constant process of upheaval and repositioning, there was no closure, and I noticed it. It often left me feeling confused and anxious. I wanted to move on to the next spot but was tired or time had run away with me. It just wasn't conducive to my wellbeing.

The new patch felt elongated and uncomfortable. Vacant and vacuous. Gone were the sparse heaths with their descending woodlarks and gone were the conifer belts with their masses of goldcrests. I realised that, for what was a large geographical area, there was a distinct lack of habitat diversity. Surprisingly, for a wetland site, there weren't any expansive reed beds or tracts of boggy ground. I longed for somewhere a bit wilder and untamed, somewhere that was freer.

There was only one area of rough grassland, attracting the occasional wheatear in spring, and it was only viewable from behind fences and gates. I missed being close to the birds, the larks singing above my head on warm days and the energy of the stonechat flicking from brush to gorse. Oh, gorse! How I missed its tropical coconut aroma enveloping me as the bright yellow flowers erupted in spring. It was this multi-sensory magic and the resident birds, so consistent in their presence, that ultimately drew me back there.

My old patch contained three individual wildlife sites: one that was small and circular in route, and two that were interconnected and sprawling. Their openness gave me those savannah-like qualities and the mental spatial openness I mentioned. Between them they featured myriad habitats: heathland, wildflower meadow, valley mire, mixed woodland, several waterbodies and masses of dense scrub. I realised that all the criteria that make an environment restorative to me interweave and cross over each other to create one overarching criterion. That a restorative environment requires a convergence of habitats and micro-environments.

The old patch beckoned me back.

The new patch was blessed with a long and regular history of wildlife monitoring and this took a sheen off my own observations, as there was very little that actually qualified as something new or significant. Obviously, this was an issue of my own making and of pure selfishness, but it still impacted on my enjoyment and connection. My old patch, once monitored, turned out to be a place of much biodiversity in both flora and fauna; however, the only documentation exploring this was an old survey report from the 1990s. This made it a blank canvas and more of an immersive challenge.

It continued to call me back.

If I hadn't been interested in analysing my experiences, then I never would've changed my patch in the first place. I really hadn't considered the impact it would have on me and I thought that, given time, my connection with a new patch would solidify like the old one. However, ten months into my year-long experiment into sense of place, this strengthening just hadn't happened. I accept that the knowledge that it was all a test may have programmed my mindset towards being stubborn and less receptive, but I discovered through a mixture of feelings and experiences that the connection I believed I felt for my old patch was a tangible thing. That sense of place was real.

I found myself compelled to reacquaint myself with some old friends at the patch that started Bird Therapy, and I was keen to explore whether going back to these places would feel as magical as when I had visited them regularly. I wondered whether they could reinvigorate my love for patch birdwatching and whether we could fall in love again. The first of these return visits was to the heath, somewhere so bleak and wild that I hadn't realised how strong my connections to it actually were.

On the drive home from work one day, I had the sudden urge to take a detour and go there. I jostled down the access track, whilst the familiar bumps and scrapes of my car reminded me of bygone days. I remembered the layout of the lumps and ridges, the judders of the suspension ingrained to memory. A third of the way down the track appeared my own private parking spot, a passing-place adjacent to the horse paddocks, empty and ready. It was still the starting point of the looping path I'd established the previous year. It hadn't changed.

It felt fantastic to be back there and as I stepped out of the car, I brimmed with ebullience. The paddock was stocked with birds; a trio of pied wagtails '*chizicked*' their way around a horse's ankles, a linnet whirred and buzzed on the wooden fence and chaffinches bounded along the hedge line. Elation! I was infused with a renewed positivity and motivation; gone were the memories of bird-less winter walks there. Banished were the negative views of the other place. I hopped the fence, buoyed by the experience of revisiting. Oh, how I'd missed this alien landscape, so dry, chalky and moonlike. How could somewhere so empty feel so full?

I walked out into the centre of the heath, where the bushes were cast open to reveal an area of short grass, resembling a fairway on a golf course. I beheld the panoramic view of the entire site that spread out from this spot and I stopped and breathed, filling my mind and lungs with the air of serenity. I felt like I'd returned home. Suddenly, my meditative state was broken by a rough '*chack*' call, emitted from directly above me.

I looked up and could see the arrowed shape of a bulky black thrush, flying low towards the distant tree line. It landed atop a small conifer – the scaly wing and remains of a white bib were unmistakable. I hadn't been here for months and was being welcomed by a bird that I'd seen here more than anywhere else, a ring ouzel. This place always had a magic feel – a magnetic pull – and it always seemed to have these birds at the right times of the year. They were a constant. It was a reminder. I shouldn't have left.

After spending some time contemplating, I decided to return to my car, and as I prepared to move, I disturbed three birds from the ground nearby. They flew cautiously up to the gorse that had grown up around the southern fence-line, and as they did, they uttered another unmistakable call – the '*tzeep*' of redwings. How I'd longed to hear this autumnal arrangement again. I'd expected this moment to occur at the Norfolk coast as they streamed in overhead, riding a strong easterly wind, and not inland, on a spartan heathland. I couldn't believe I'd spent so long away; I was jubilant and I felt like my connection had been plugged back in again. This was the end of my absence. My return to the heath.

There are many approaches to birdwatching and whilst I've explored lots of these in depth, I must be clear that there are still some angles I haven't sampled. Every birdwatcher takes something different from their hobby and I've observed many positive, and also negative, attitudes towards it. Through talking to people and via my survey, several approaches seem to be the most popular and these are the *modus operandi* I've mainly focused on: twitching, patching, surveying, listing, observing garden birds and finding rare birds.

Given my experiences with twitching and my mental health, I wasn't overly surprised that only sixty-five people in the entire survey stated they engaged with it. Interestingly, six people were keen to point out that they no longer twitched – perhaps even more pertinent in a chapter about an evolving and changing hobby. Eighty-five people described themselves as patch 'watchers', or as regular visitors to their local patches. Twenty-four people mentioned the word 'survey' in their responses and for me, the most surprising result from the survey was that an astonishing 124 people kept a list of some description. Although many seemed keen to add that these were purely just for referential purposes.

Over the past year, I've stopped keeping a year list myself. As well as being an experiment as part of my writing, it has also been a way of reconnecting with the outdoors on a more spiritual level, and it removed that underlying urgency to move on and try to see more. I still keep records of what I see and these are an important part of my own connection with nature – they're my mapping, my emotional spreadsheet; but by removing numbers from birdwatching, unless it's for a WeBS count, I've found that it simplifies the entire process of engaging with it. Much like the survey, my own lists are purely for reference and data gathering, not one-upmanship and competition.

To ensure some objectivity in my assessment of birdwatching approaches, I posed a question on social media about the different approaches to birdwatching that people recognised and engaged with. I received some excellent responses, which validated the categories I'd already identified; however, several others were mentioned that I'd overlooked. There are so many ways to engage with it, and in the same way that we're all different, as birdwatchers we all approach our experiences from different perspectives.

There can also be extenuating factors that impact our engagement. For example, you may not possess the particular skillset required to undertake a certain approach. Many people within my research stated that they find great joy and solitude in sketching and painting birds – but this requires a certain level of artistic adroitness, in order to truly engage with it. Some approaches are still inaccessible for people with physical disabilities or impairment, and yes, there is great joy to be found in watching and listening to garden birds closer to home, but frustratingly, some larger nature reserves still remain unsuitable for people with mobility issues.

Preserving localised green spaces and making them open to all simply needs to be a priority, both locally and nationally. On a positive note, I've visited a few reserves recently that have newly constructed hides and boardwalks designed to increase accessibility. It's good to see nature and conservation organisations making the adjustments they should to promote inclusion and engagement.

Other approaches might require access to more specialist equipment. Recently there's been a small revolution in technological birdwatching approaches, with one flagship format being 'nocmig'. Short for nocturnal migration, nocmig is the act of sound recording overnight and then listening back, usually through a computer, to see if you can hear and identify any flyover bird calls.

In fact, there's been several occasions when the Norfolk-wide network of birdwatchers on social media have reported vast numbers of birds calling over their homes on foggy nights. It's exciting to know that there may be something utterly random passing above and I've been unable to resist inquisitively poking my head outside to listen. There's something wonderfully surreal about standing out in your own garden, swallowed up by the pitch-black night air, as the mournful calls of migrating waders pass overhead. I had a similar, ethereal experience one January evening, when a dense descent of dewy fog had smothered our town. It was so heavy that it made everything feel a bit claustrophobic and our willow ended up draped with a grey veil.

Later that evening, I received a message from a friend, telling me that I should go outside and listen to the pink-footed geese passing overhead. I'd never seen or heard pink feet flying over our town, so I stepped out of the sliding doors in anticipation. I knew I wouldn't be able to see their angular 'flying-v' skein formations, but I hoped to hear their noisy honking instead. Oh, I certainly heard them alright. A chorus of cackling honks, nervous and urgent, sounding like they were scared of the low fog that was disorientating them. It was bizarre to stand amidst this cacophony, and even more so when a lone goose passed close above me, only metres away.

Another approach that lots of people suggested to me was bird photography, which for many now is a fundamental element of modern birdwatching. With advances in mobile technology, smartphones now feature high-quality cameras and they also sit well on most optical equipment, to act as pseudo zoom lenses. This makes bird photography more accessible, as do the newer digital SLR and bridge cameras. Photographers seem to occasionally cause friction at birdwatching sites and it appears that they can be viewed as a nuisance, with many people complaining about them trying to get closer to their quarry for the best shot.

I guess the key point here is that we all have different motivations for our bird and nature experiences, and finding an equilibrium that suits all will always be an unlikely outcome. Most birdwatchers now carry a camera or a smartphone with one built in, therefore most birdwatchers are photographers in the widest sense of the word. It's an interesting conundrum and one that isn't going to go away.

What all of this does, though, is overcomplicate what should be a simple pastime. It adds unnecessary padding to an already multi-layered hobby. It strips away some of the essence of what makes people fall in love with birdwatching in the first place. All of my most rewarding and rejuvenating birdwatching experiences have been when I've adopted a 'back-to-basics' attitude and embraced the primal awe of nature and the outdoors.

I'm all for connecting with people, but if you become immersed in the culture and subculture of birdwatching then things can change and often dramatically so. Expectations and motivations can shift and perceived pressures can arise, such as the pressure to find birds, to report them immediately and to see as many of them as possible. These 'rules' may be self-imposed but may also be influenced by the attitudes and behaviours of other people. Unfortunately, what should in essence be a positive, relaxing and connective hobby can sometimes become negative, anxiety-inducing and divisive. There have been times when I've seen birdwatchers clash on social media over unshared sightings of rare birds, in a cardinal birdwatching sin known as 'suppression'. There are often valid reasons for doing this though, usually around access rights or site sensitivity.

Yes, technology has changed the landscape of birdwatching, but not always for the better. I've witnessed numerous exchanges on social media that have verged on bullying and they're often just because someone got something wrong or suppressed a bird. On the plus side, with more birdwatchers using social media to share their observations, information is much more readily available generally increasing accessibility and opportunity.

However, even this can have a negative impact, as rare bird news spreads like wildfire, fuelling some people's urgency to see a particular bird. This can lead to the disrespecting of the wishes of landowners, as seen at a recent Norfolk twitch, where birdwatchers were seen crossing into private land to view a rare bird. It's no wonder then that birdwatchers suppress sightings on private land, especially when they may have worked hard to build trust with local landowners, as I had to with my own patch. This is all a bit of a negative cycle, illustrated recently when a birdwatcher shared with me that they felt depressed at missing out on seeing a rare bird, due to it being suppressed. I expressed my view: that I felt it was unwise for them to have attached such significance to something so far out of their control. A bird is a wild and free creature after all.

Through the years of writing and research, one simple message has repeatedly cropped up, and that's the idea of a back-to-basics approach to birdwatching. To remove all of the elements that can make it negative and to just accept the avian world around us, in its rawest form. The 'basics' here are the birds, our senses and our feelings, and this is how Bird Therapy changed for me and how my hobby came full-circle. I started out by wanting to know and experience everything. An approach which, although I don't regret, took me away from the foundations of the hobby and off on various tangents, until I fell back into it without expectation.

By peeling off these layers, you become more attuned to the intrinsic power and energy of nature as it unfolds around you. I urge you to take a step back, leave technology behind, stop actively searching for birds and simply allow yourself to be present, in their company. Watch them with your eyes, perceive them with every sense, and please just try being at one with birds and nature.

If you're already a birdwatcher, then I hope this book has offered you an alternative viewpoint into your hobby. I've tried to pick apart and then stitch back together the things that make our shared interest so wonderful. Perhaps my words have consolidated what you always thought about birdwatching but may have never truly considered: its healing power and the web of wonder it weaves around all those who partake in it.

If you're thinking of taking up birdwatching as a hobby, then I hope this book has given you some ideas on how to get started and some of the various ways you can engage with it. If you've approached in a more generalised nature, or from a mental health perspective, I hope that my experiences and openness have been engaging and that you feel you can apply my five ways to well-birding to your outdoor experiences.

If you're a policymaker, an influencer, or perhaps you work at a nature or health organisation, then please share the messages in this book. Tell people about it, show it to others and help to spread the word about how birdwatching can help us with our mental health and wellbeing. Introduce people to the five ways to well-birding, the multi-sensory wonder of nature and the consistency of a garden bird community – of any bird community. One day I hope that our doctors will be able to prescribe sessions of birdwatching and I will continue spreading my own wings to help this happen.

When I introduced the concept of Bird Therapy, I said I hoped to present a compelling case for the therapeutic benefits of birdwatching. In these final paragraphs as I reflect on my writing, I feel like I might just have done that. I've realised that Bird Therapy is a genuine thing now, and not just a concept. More people have been in contact with me than ever, thanking me for my writing and for helping them with their own troubles, but don't thank me – thank the birds.

Whilst Bird Therapy is obviously about birdwatching, it's also about the way it has enhanced and improved my wellbeing and that of others. One of the most obvious changes that I associate with birdwatching is the positive transformation in my identity, my metamorphosis if you like. The lifestyle changes that I made in the period before embarking on the process of 'sorting myself out' resulted in the fizzling out of many aspects of my life. These included dramatic changes in my career direction and my social interactions – the fundamental elements of my personal identity.

Throughout school I identified as the 'clever naughty kid' and this formed the crux of my identity outside of it. In my teenage years I was rarely on my own and I suppose that this was a direct result of the feelings of loss and being lost that I experienced through my formative years. I hated being alone and I hated feeling removed or distant from social situations. Therefore, I pushed myself to the front of every group in every way that I could and often got myself into trouble by doing so. There's a huge void in my life, where I wasted many years pumping my body and mind with various poisons, in the belief that I was actually enjoying myself. The irony is that these were my lowest times but I just couldn't see it, let alone accept it.

Birdwatching gave me an opportunity to embrace the 'geek within' and accept who I really am. It also helped me to create a positive focus for my obsessive tendencies and, in embarking on Bird Therapy, a way of adopting a positive persona after years of negativity. I know I have a strong sense of identity and I'm proud that I can talk about my hobby and my mental health and can challenge some of the traditionally negative stereotypes of both. As I've shared throughout this book, the more that I've learned about myself, the more I've learned about the world around me and how, with every change that occurs in life, the constancy of nature underpins everything.

Writing this book has been a phenomenal experience too. My style and approach haven't changed, but the way I write certainly has. It's been cathartic to reflect back on more difficult times and connect them with the natural moments that eased them. As my words became stronger, I felt empowered to share my message and story, in the hope that it may help and inspire other people too.

Along with other lifestyle changes I've made and support I've received since I've been birdwatching, I've been able to regulate my feelings and responses to stress in a much more appropriate way. I feel like I can rationalise my thoughts more sensibly now, and whilst this isn't a direct result of birdwatching, I'm certain that it's helped. The fact that I have multiple escape routes and safe havens that I can go to when I'm struggling has helped me to level out and compartmentalise my issues and worries.

This works in tandem with the stability and calmness that I gain from nature and birdwatching. Stripping back my senses to engage with the simplistic beauty of nature has fostered an intrinsically mindful approach to every moment spent outdoors. These times of connection and reflection have given me opportunities to understand myself and my thoughts in non-judgemental and restorative environments – pulling together all the strands that make Bird Therapy what it is. A journey that I hope will never end – for me and anyone else that embarks on it.

Consistent and constant, yet wild and free
Are the avian wonders comforting me.
From the lake at my patch, to the gorse-speckled heath,
they dowse me in light, over darkness beneath.
Sharpening senses, they help me to find,
the systems and solace that strengthen my mind.
From meadow to estuary, shingle to tree,
I'll always be thankful for Bird Therapy.

Notes

I

1. *Oxford English Dictionary* website, 'Main definitions of *hawk* in English' at https://en.oxforddictionaries.com/definition/hawk
2. Peter Allard, Don Dorling, Michael Seago and Moss Taylor, *The Birds of Norfolk*, Pica Press, East Sussex, 1999, p. 44.

II

1. © Mind. This information is published in full at mind.org.uk
2. *Ibid.*
3. *Ibid.*
4. Kevin Fenton, Public Health England, © Mind. 'Feel better outside, feel better inside: Ecotherapy for mental wellbeing, resilience and recovery', 2013, p 3.

III

1. Dr William Bird for the RSPB, 'Natural Thinking', 1st edn, 2007, pp. 33–35.

2. Mihaly Csikszentmihalyi, *Flow and the Foundations of Positive Psychology: The Collected Works of Mihaly Csikszentmihaly*, Springer, Dordrecht, 2014, pp. 135–152.

IV

1. King's College London website, 'Study suggests exposure to trees, the sky and birdsong in cities beneficial for mental wellbeing' at https://www.kcl. ac.uk/ioppn/news/records/2018/january/study-suggests-exposure-to-trees-the-sky-and-birdsong-in-cities-beneficial-for-mental-wellbeing.aspx

2. Eleanor Ratcliffe et al., 'Bird sounds and their contributions to perceived attention restoration and stress recovery', *Journal of Environmental Psychology*, Elsevier, New York, 2013, p. 7.

3. Michael Guida, 'Britain's Sonic Therapy: listening to birdsong during and after the First World War' at https://remedianetwork.net/2015/06/16/britains-sonic-therapy-listening-to-birdsong-during-and-after-the-first-world-war/

4. Paul O'Prey (ed.), *First World War Poems from the Front*, Imperial War Museum, London, 2014.

V

1. Mental Health Foundation website, 'Physical health and mental health' at https://www.mentalhealth.org.uk/a-to-z/p/physical-health-and-mental-health

2. *Oxford English Dictionary* website, 'Definition of *connect* in English' at https://en.oxforddictionaries.com/definition/connect

3. Bonita L. McFarlane, 'Specialization and Motivations of Birdwatchers', *Wildlife Society Bulletin*, 22, 1994, pp. 361–370.

4. Jon Kabat-Zinn, 'Mindfulness-Based Interventions in Context: Past, Present, and Future', *Clinical Psychology: Science and Practice,* vol. 10, issue 2. John Wiley & Sons, Summer 2003, pp. 144-156.

VI

1. Mental Health Foundation website, 'Doing good? Altruism and wellbeing in an age of austerity' at https://www.mentalhealth.org.uk/publications/doing-good-altruism-and-wellbeing-age-austerity

2. Daniel T. C. Cox and Kevin J. Gaston, 'Urban Bird Feeding: Connecting People with Nature', *PLOS ONE* at https://doi.org/10.1371/journal.pone.0158717, July 18, 2016

3. *National Geographic* website, 'Citizen science' at https://www.nationalgeographic.org/encyclopedia/citizen-science/

4. Larissa Rainey, 'The Search for Purpose in Life: An Exploration of Purpose, the Search Process, and Purpose Anxiety', University of Pennsylvania Scholarly Commons, 2014

VII

1. Gilbert White, *The Natural History of Selborne,* Unicorn Press, London, 2015.

2. Stephen Moss, *A Bird in the Bush: A Social History of Birdwatching,* Aurum Press, London, 2004, p. 14.

3. Dr William Bird for the RSPB, 'Natural Thinking', 1st edn, 2007, pp. 35–6.

4. RSPB website, 'Strumpshaw Fen' at https://www.rspb.org.uk/reserves-and-events/reserves-a-z/strumpshaw-fen/

5. Bird, 'Natural Thinking', p. 35.

6. *Ibid.* pp. 35–36.

7. *Ibid.* p. 20.

8. S.M. Low, 'Symbolic Ties That Bind' In: Irwin Altman and Setha M. Low (eds), *Place Attachment. Human Behavior and Environment (Advances in Theory and Research)*, vol 12. at https://doi.org/10.1007/978-1-4684-8753-4_8, Springer, Boston, MA, 1992

9. Jennifer E. Cross, 'What is Sense of Place?' at http://western.edu/sites/default/files/documents/cross_headwatersXII.pdf

VIII

1. Gilbert White, *The Natural History of Selborne,* Unicorn Press, London, 2015, p. 119.

IX

1. Gilbert White, *The Natural History of Selborne,* Unicorn Press, London, 2015, p. 62.

X

1. Peter Davis, 'The great immigration of early September 1965', *British Birds*, vol. 59, no. 9, 1966, pp. 353-376.

XI

1. NHS Choices website, 'Benefits of exercise' at https://www.nhs.uk/live-well/exercise/exercise-health-benefits/
2. *Oxford English Dictionary* website, 'Definition of *active* in English' at https://en.oxforddictionaries.com/definition/active
3. Walking for Health website, 'Walking Works' at https://www.walkingforhealth.org.uk/get-walking/walking-works
4. Jo Barton and Jules Pretty, 'What is the best dose of nature and green exercise for mental health? A multi-study analysis', *Environmental Science & Technology*, 44, 2010, pp. 3947–3955.
5. Harvard Health Publishing, Harvard Medical School, '6 simple steps to keep your mind sharp at any age', excerpted from *Healthbeat* (© 2018) Harvard

University, at https://www.health.harvard.edu/mind-and-mood/6-simple-steps-to-keep-your-mind-sharp-at-any-age

6. NHS Choices website, 'Keep your brain active' at https://www.nhs.uk/news/neurology/keep-your-brain-active/

7. Denise C. Park et al., 'The Impact of Sustained Engagement on Cognitive Function in Older Adults: The Synapse Project' at https://www.ncbi.nlm.nih.gov/pmc/articles/PMC4154531/

8. Diana Bowler, Lisette M. Buyung-Ali, Teri M. Knight and Andrew Pullin, 'A systematic review of evidence for the added benefits to health of exposure to natural environments', *BMC Public Health*, 10. 456.

XII

1. NHS Choices website, 'Learn for mental wellbeing' at https://www.nhs.uk/conditions/stress-anxiety-depression/learn-for-mental-wellbeing/

2. Geoff Petty, *Teaching Today: A Practical Guide*, 4th edn, Nelson Thornes Ltd, Cheltenham, 2009, p. 336.

3. John Law and Michael Lynch, 'Lists, field guides, and the descriptive organization of seeing: Birdwatching as an exemplary observational activity', *Human Studies*, 11, Kluwer Academic Publishers, 1988, pp. 271–303.

4. Petty, *Teaching Today*, p. 213.

5. Institute for Outdoor Learning website, 'What is

Outdoor Learning' at https://www.outdoor-learning-research.org/Research/What-is-Outdoor-Learning

The survey questions

1. Do you have a diagnosed mental health condition?
   (yes/no)
2. Please share details of Q1. (open answer)
3. Have you received or are you still receiving any
   treatment for this condition and if so what was/is it?
   (e.g. talking therapy, medication)
4. On a scale of 1–5, how much would you say that your
   mental health affects your *daily* life? (never/not often/
   occasionally/often/all the time)
5. In a typical week, how many hours do you spend
   birding? (1–5/5–10/10–20/20–30/30–50/50+)
6. On the scale below, please state how seriously you
   take birding. (recreationally/hobby/passionately/
   competitively/obsessively)
7. Please state below what you do when you go out
   birding. Please be as detailed and specific as possible.
   For example, if you watch birds, list them, twitch them
   and so on. (open answer)
8. Do you bird a specific patch or multiple locations?
   Please give details. (open answer)

9. Finally, please use the space below to share what it is about birding that you believe has helped you with your mental health and wellbeing. Please be as detailed as possible. (open answer)

Acknowledgements

I'd like to thank: Pops for being my inspiration; my partner Emma, for allowing me to enjoy my hobby and putting up with me talking about this book relentlessly – I promise that it's now finished. Mum, David and all my grandparents for their love and support. Kieran for everything he helped me with and the experiences we shared, many of which shaped this book. Tim, Dave and John for providing me with excellent constructive feedback on my writing. Jim for sharing my ethos and for loving East Norfolk. Sacha and Johnny for their friendship and company. Steve for the experiences, support and encouragement when I first started writing. Vanessa at Diane's Pantry for the exquisite coffee. Will and Kayn for the shared experiences in this book. James for identifying anything for me, at any time; you really are a phenomenal naturalist. All of the 'Valley of Kings'. The management and residents at my patch for allowing me to have unprecedented access to the park. Wensum Valley Birdwatching Society for always making me feel welcome. The Norfolk Wildlife Trust and the RSPB for maintaining their local reserves. Opticron for kindly providing me with excellent optics. Simon for initially believing in this book and acting as a sounding board throughout. Unbound for making this book real and for their support from the beginning. Jo for being the most talented illustrator I've ever seen. Chris Packham for writing the foreword and helping to spread the message. Tina for sprinkling fairy dust and making good things happen. Chris and Team4Nature for their unprecedented and constant support from the early days. Mark Avery and David Callahan for multiple opportunities to share my work. Patrick Barkham for the fantastic writing advice. Everyone that writes and tweets about the benefits of birdwatching and nature for mental health. Perhaps most importantly, I'd like to thank everybody who has shared their feelings, experiences, anecdotes and opinions with me; face to face, through my survey and via Twitter.

I extend special thanks to all who pledged to make this book not just a dream, but a reality. Especially Deb Jordan, Bill Bailey and Adam Huttly for their generous patronage.

Unbound is the world's first crowdfunding publisher, established in 2011.

We believe that wonderful things can happen when you clear a path for people who share a passion. That's why we've built a platform that brings together readers and authors to crowdfund books they believe in – and give fresh ideas that don't fit the traditional mould the chance they deserve.

This book is in your hands because readers made it possible. Everyone who pledged their support is listed below. Join them by visiting unbound.com and supporting a book today.

Aisha
Liz Albert
Juliette Aldous
Katherine Alker
David Allan
Lisa Allsop
Alison Anderson
Tamsin Andrews
Alison Archibald
Kate Argyle
Shaun Arkley
Rebecca Armstrong
Julie Arnold
Catherine Artindale
Colin Ashcroft
Kate Ashley

Francesca Ashurst
Bill Aspin
Neil Atkinson
Mark Avery
Nick Avery
Ron Baber
David Bailey
Kit Bailey
Richard Bailey-Jones
Stefan Bainbridge
Becky Baines
Debby Baker
P. Bakker
Chris Balchin
Laura Baldwin
Phil Ball

Paul Bamford
Debbie Banyard
Sacha Barbato
Nicholas Barber
Caroline Barlow
Debbie Barnes
Janine Barnett-Phillips
Jo Baron
Niall Barr
Amy Barrett
Jill Barrett
Zoe Barrett
Simon Barsby
Kiri Barson
Anne Bartlett
Jane Barton
Lesley Bassett
Virginia Bassett
Betzi Bateman
Ginny Battson
Emma Bayliss
Heidi Bayliss
Val Bayliss-Brideaux
Jane Beaton
Catherine Beck
Clare Beck
Jane Bellerby
Vidya Bellur
Kerry Bennett
Anita Benson
David Bernstein
Kay Berrill
Stewart Betts
Karen Beynon
John Billings
Adam Bimpson

Jo Birch
Jan Bird
Jane Bird
Callum Black
Vicki Blair
Claire Blennerhassett
Poppy Azumi Bliss
Liam Blizard
Margaret Bluman
Anthony Blunden
Beth Bodycote
Catherine Bolt
Tabatha Boniface
Stacey Booth
Brian Boothby
David Borthwick
Catherine Bowles
Debra Bowles
Sarah Box
John Boyce
Brian Boyle
Richard Bradford
Jim Bradley
James Brennan
Kelly Brenner
Gabrielle Bretherton
Katie Bridger
Adrian Briggs
Paul Brook
Rebecca Brook
Emma Brooks
Anne Brophy
Donna Brown
Graeme Brown
Jackie Brown
Lotti Brown

Marianne Brown
Jo Brown (TAOJB)
Janine Brown Jones
Isabel Bryony
Catherine Buck
Stuart Buck
Adam & Rebecca Buckley
Elaine Buckton
Kirsty Buhler
Alison Bunning
Les Bunyan
Dylan Burgess
Sarah Burgess
Steve Burnett
Pat Burton
Malcolm Busby
Beaujolais Bussell
Hannah Butcher
Jack Butlin
Jeffrey Butterworth
Ian Byrne
Andy Cage
Alison Cameron
Sharon Campbell
Anna Canetty-Clarke
David Canning
John Cantelo
JoAnn Carlson
Steve Carnaby
Gail Carr
Liz Carr
David Carrier
Laura Carter
Jon Cartledge
Bruce Caswell
Mike Challis

Stephen Chapman
Paul Cheney
Carl Clare
Heather Clare
Dr. Christina Blume Clark
Jeanne Clark
Jeremy Clark
Thomas Clark
Jill Clarke
Stephen Clarke
Sarah Louise Cleary
Cley Spy Ltd
Allison Clough
Clare Cochrane
Lauren Cockburn
Thomas Cogley
Becky Coles
Martin Collins
Michael "Buzz" Collins
Diane Collinson
Mary Colwell
Joseph Connor
Anne Cooper
Claire Cooper
Tommy Corcoran
Ellie Cornell
Michelle Cornish
Dermot Cosgrove
Lisa Cotton
Peter Cotton
Ed Coulson
Ade Couper
Martin Court
Amaryllis Courtney
Dominic Couzens
Jane Cowan

Robert Cox
Sally Crosland
Julia Croyden
Corinne Cruickshank
Haymar Da Silva
Annamarie Dack
Joanne Dalton
Neil Daly
Joseph Dance
Kevin Dance
Ralph Darvill
Jonathan Davidson
Kathryn Davie
Claire Davies
William Davies
Andrew Davis
Gemma Davis
Bob Dawson
Kath Dawson
Nigel De Wit
Tim Dee
James Dennett
Pete Dennis
Liz Dexter
Kirsten Dickson
James Disley
Richard Dobbins
Gavin Donnelly
Richard Doran-Sherlock
Andrew Dove
Katy Driver
Peter Driver
@drmikefraser
Rebekah Drury
Ian Duckett
Steve Dudley

Alison Duncan
Shirley Dunlop
Joanne Dunn
Ryan Dunn
John Dunne
Daniel Durling
Neil Dyson
Anders E
Mel Ede
Phil Edwards
Anna Efimova
Lesley Elliott
Natasha Ellison
James Emerson
Mike Erskine
Cath Evans
Ieuan Evans
Simon Evans
Jamie Everett
Gary Eyer
John Fanshawe
Charles Farrell
Virginia Fassnidge
Peter Faulkner
John Ferguson
Tracey Fernandes
Benne Ferrell
Yvonne Findlay
Alexia Fishwick
Matt, Natalie & Poppie
    Fitzmaurice
Dan Fletcher
Caroline Foot
Angela Ford
Chris Foster
Sabine Foster

Neil Fox
Jon Frampton
Olly Frampton
Helen Franklin
Matthew Franklin
Scott Franklin
Robin Fransham
David Frost
Jacqui Frost
Mark Frost
Carol Fry
Nicola Fry
Katie Fuller
Mary Galbraith
Abigail Gallivan
Hilary Gallo
Majda Gama
Nicholas Garforth
Kieran Garland
Owen Garling
Gillian Gatiss
Deborah Gatty
Rebekah Gawthorpe
Martin George
Bruno Girin
Mark Goggins
Rob Going
Sophie Goldsworthy
Heidi Good
Roberta Goodall
Roo Goodwin
Steve Gore
Marie Grainger
Debbie Grantham
Nicola Greer
Julie Grewer

Ed Griffin
David Griffiths
Ray Griffiths
Claire Grinham
Marie Grint
Elaine Ground
Tracy Gunn
Kevin Guttridge
Chris Hackett
Matt Hadlington
Maggie Hage
Adrian Hall
Sophie Hall
Laurell Hamilton
Edward Hancox
Lisa Hardi
Kate Hardie
Melissa Harding
Jeanie Hardman
Sam Hardy
Stewart Hares
Evelyn Hargraves
Robin Hargreaves
Kath Harley
Charlotte Harris Cook
Jennie Harrod
Paul G Harrop
Vicky Hartigan
Alison Harvey
James Harvey
Tim Harwood
Kathleen Hassall
Dave Hawkins
Jonathan Hawkins
Matthew Hawthorne
James Heal

Helen Hedderick
Fergus Henderson
Mhairi Henderson
Rachel Henderson
Sam Hicks
Jane Higgins
Jeremy Hill
Grace Hillard
Karen Hinckley
Judy Hindle
Beth Hiscock
Greg Hitchcock
Sam Hockaday
Daniel Hodgkin
Dennis Hollinghurst
Rob Holmes
Mark Hopson
Janet Hoptroff
Gaynor Horton
Jane Hoskyn
Claire Houle
Chris Howard
Jo Howard
Ian Howat
Tracy Howells
Rachel Hoyes
Sean Huggins
Anthony Hughes
Liz Hughes
Marc Hughes
Rebekah Hughes
Pete Humphrey
Terry Hunter
Andy Hurley
Eleanor Hurley
Fiona Hussey

Mark Hutchinson
Ian and Ruth
Trevor Ingman
Jamie Ingrouille
Deryck Irving
J.D.
Edward Jackson
Abi Jacobs
Warren Jacques
Phil James
Robert James
Wendy James
Wil Jarmain
Barry Jarvie
Jemma
Linda Jerrom
Kit Jewitt
Emily Joáchim
Alice Johnson
Louise Johnson
Pete Johnson
Harvey Jones
Lesley Jones
Pea Jones
Sian Jones
Stephen Jones
Stephen and Danni
    Jorgenson-Murray
John Judge
Paul Jupp
Joanne K
Emma Kane
Stella Kane
Kathryn & Stephen
Melissa Katsoulis
Ed Keeble

Jo Keeley
Liz Kennea
Christina Kennedy
Lucie Kennedy
Dan Kenny
Louise Kerr Ilett
Edward Kerrison
Jan Kewley
Dan Kieran
John Kilner
Janneke Kimstra
Amy King
Laura King
Sally-Ann King
Lana Kirczenow
Alison Kirkman
Art & Margie Klein
Angela Knight
Ian Knight
Pooky Knightsmith
Jeff Knott
Michaela Knowles
Emily Knox
Natalie Kober
Daniel Kronenberg
Sheryl La Bouchardiere
Nichola Lamkin
Alex Large
Renée Lascala
Liam Lavelle
Ron Lawie
Conrad Lawrence
Geoff Laws
Kim Le Patourel
Debbie Lee
Robert Lee

Tom Lee
Maryline Leese
Eugene Lefeuvre
Mary Lester
Anne Leuchars
Ceri Levy
James Lidster
Tina Lindsay
Barbara Litza
LizTRON
Abbie Loader
Carey Lodge
Michelle Lomas
Lomelindrie
Sarah Long
Tom Lord
Claudia Lowe
Fiona Macalister
Bill Macdonald
Robert MacDonald
Robert Macfarlane
Andrew MacGarvey
Ross Mackenzie
Seonaid Mackenzie-Murray
Iona Macphie
Graeme Madden
Christine Maddock
Laura Maddox
Jo Makowski
Richard Malton
Elliott Mannis
MarGinsWalkandGlamp
Naomi Markham
Maggie Marriott
Ken Marsden
Sarah Marshall

Vikki Marshall
Rosie Marteau
Geoff Martin
Pete Martin
Lucinda Marturano
Kim Matthews
Rose Matthews
Shirley Mawer
Darren Mayer
Linda Mayhew
Kevin Mc Quillan
Kari McBride
Douglas McCabe
Helen McCallin
Angela McCann
Lucy McCarry
Mike McCarthy
Kate McCormack
Martine McDonagh
Gary McGee
Chris McGregor
Kevin McGregor
Miranda McGregor
Roley McIntyre
Fiona McKenna
Sarah McKinlay
Sara McMahon
Alison McMillan
Geoffrey McMullan
Kirsteen McNish
Angela Meekins
Julie Meikle
Carl Mesner Lyons
Simon Metcalfe
Wendy Mewes
Fatima Mharchat

Dr. Ian Middlebrook
Laura Middlebrook
@mindfulwalks
Dominic Mitchell
Michelle Mitchell
John Mitchinson
Deena Mobbs
Salim Mohammed
Hannah Molyneaux
Richard Montagu
Chris Moore
David Moore
Linda Moore
Charles Morgan
Jonathan Morgan
Rosemary Morgan
Trish Morgan
T Morley
Liz Morris
Morris Morris
P Morris
Marie Morrison
Robert Morrison
Polly Mortimer
Stephen Moss
Caroline Mountain
Ben Mullard
Catherine Munro
Diane Murphy
Emma Murphy
Jane Murphy
Stephanie Murphy
David Murray
Carlo Navato
David Neal
Andrew Neave

Nicola Nestor
Jackie Newcombe
Sarah Newton-Scott
Rachel Niblock
Lucy Nichol
Natalie Nichols
Simon Niederberger
Sue Nieland
Rachel Nightingale
Mark Noble
Stuart Noble
Katharine Norbury
Jen Nutbeem
Ann O'Dea
Adeline Patricia O'Keeffe
Patrick O'Neill
Proinsias O'Tuama
Sarah Oates
Sean Offord
Tara Okon
Jenna Oppenheimer
Howard Orridge
Steve Orridge
Mike Owens
Rachael Page
Lucy Palfreyman
Wendy Palmer-Grove
Yi Pang
Lev Parikian
Kate Parker
Sarah Parker
Nicky Parkinson
Rob Parsons
Alex Parsons-Hulse
Lin Pateman
Andy Paton

Emma Payne
Mark Peachey
Susannah Pearse
Jessica Pennock
Suzanne Penny
Hugo Perks
Stuart Petch
Charity A. Petrov
Bob Philpott
Laura Philpott
Phil Pickin
S Pickles
Grant Pickup
Laura Pictor
Chris Platt
Jacqueline Pluck
Steve Pocock
Justin Pollard
Kara Ponsford
Steve Pont
Katrina Poole
Kristopher Poole
Alison Pope
Beki Pope
Rob Pople
Joanne Porter
Mike Porter
Tabitha Potts
Michael Priaulx
Neil Price
Matt Pringle
Sarah Purton
Diane Puterbaugh
Lisa Quattromini
Alex Rafinski
Ramblinglea

Patrick Ramsey
Alex Randall
Jonny Rankin
Christina Ravinet
Gareth Redmond-King
Alison Rees
Jamie Regan
Lara Reid
Ruth Revell
Chris Revett
Dan Rewcastle
Lesley Rhodes
Jan Riché
Loralee Richter
Kate Risely
Jennifer Roberts
Angus Robin
Raine Robinson
Rachael Rodway
Josie Rogers
Niki Rogers
Robyn Roscoe
Peter Rossiter
Dominic Rothwell
David Rouse
Chris Routh
Adrian Rowe
Carole Rowe
Darren Royle
Björn Rulik
Alistair Rush
Fiona Russell
Lindsay Russell
Nick Rutter
Catherine Rye
Claire Sallows

Emma Salt
Ryan Sampson
Christoph Sander
Gill Sapsed
Chad Sarles
John Saunders
Kirsty Sawtell
Denise Schofield
Freda Scott-Park
ScruffApple
Paul Seeney
Pete Selwood
Kasper Seward
Helen Sewell
Karen Shakespeare and
    Ziggy
Carl Shanks
Ashlea Shaw
Ian Sherriffs
Amarjeet Sian
Lorna Simes
Mike Simmonds
David Simpkin
Tony Sinnott
Jonathan Sly
Chris Small
Penny Smallshire
Corinna Smart
Karin Smerdon
Dawn Smith
Helen Smith
Immy Smith
Michael Smith
Paul Smith
Phil Smith
Philip Smith

Robin Smith
Sam Smith
Simon Smith
Therese Smith
Roseanne Soong
Murray Spear
Linda Spence
Ralph Sperring
Mark Spokes
Mandy Stanton
Rob Stephens
Sue Stephenson-Martin
Julie Stevenson
Mandy Stokes
Alexander Stone
Nick Stone
Ruth Stone
Houghton Mary Strand
Brigit Strawbridge
Kerry Stubbs
Claire Sturgess
Richard Sulley
Alan Summers
Claire Sutherland
Jackie Swann
Marion Sweeney
Katie Swords
Diana Tahourdin
Amanda Tall
Pip Tallents
Pip & Muriel Tallents
Claire Taylor
Jo Taylor
Laura Taylor Innes
Emma Taylor Johnson
Nigel Teece

Chris Thomas
Gerwyn Thomas
Matt Thomas
Richard Thomas
Rosie Thomas
Will Thomas
Helen Thompson
Inge Thomson
Clare Thorp
Katie Thorpe
Gwynneth Threlfall
Mr & Mrs Tig
Jenny Tither
Dale Tomaselli
Sarah Tookey
Sabine Tötemeyer
Madeleine Totham
Lindsay Trevarthen
Rebecca Tucker
Robin Tuddenham
Hannah Tunnard
Justin Tunstall
Chris Turner
Jo Turner
Wayne Robert Turner
Kit Turton
Ian Ulyatt
Stu Vallance
Barend van Gemerden
Annemarie van Ommen
Charlotte Varela
Jennifer Vaudin
Alan Venables
Dr. Johnny Vere-Hodge
Deborah Vittori Garman
John Wadkin

Tom Wait
Marek Walford
Sarah Walker-Guy
Gill Walmsley
Ben Walsh
Declan Walsh
Louise Walters
Catherine Ward
Graham Jeffrey Ward
Elizabeth (Liz) Ware
Edwina Watson
John Watson
Miranda Watson
Sarah Watson
Becky Webb
Rowena Wells
Janice Welsh
Anna Wesener
Richard West
Anthony Wetherhill
Graham White
Heloise White
Edin Whitehead
Miranda Whiting
Richard Whiting
Tina Whitley
Susan Wilde

Lucy Wilkins
Victoria Wilkinson
Chris Williams
Donna Williams
Nick Williams
Rosie Williams
Mike Willis
Helen Wilson
Richard Wise
Howard Wix
Catherine Wood
Matt Wood
Martin Wood-Weatherill
Alison Woodward
Barbara Wright
Jamie Wyver
Sally Yallop
Paul Yarrow
Alison Yates
Angela Yates
Kristie Yorkston
Andy Young
Ian Young
Richard Young
Nigel Youngman
Donna Zimmer